Academic
Learning
Series

# Managing a
Microsoft®
# Windows® 2000
## Network Environment

## Lab Manual

PUBLISHED BY
Microsoft Press
A Division of Microsoft Corporation
One Microsoft Way
Redmond, Washington 98052-6399

Copyright © 2002 by Microsoft Corporation.

Library of Congress Cataloging-in-Publication Data
MCSA Training Kit : Managing a Microsoft Windows 2000 Network Environment (Exam 70-218) / Microsoft Corporation.
        p. cm.
   Includes index.
   ISBN 0-7356-1581-0
   ISBN 0-7356-1773-2 (Academic Learning Series)
   ISBN 0-07-285086-8 (McGraw-Hill Ryerson)
   1. Electronic data processing personnel--Certification.  2. Microsoft software--Examinations--Study guides.  3. Microsoft Windows (Computer file).  I. Microsoft Corporation.

QA76.3 .M3266  2002
005.4'4769--dc21                          2001057971

Printed and bound in the United States of America.

1 2 3 4 5 6 7 8 9   QWT   7 6 5 4 3 2

Distributed by McGraw-Hill Ryerson.

A CIP catalogue record for this book is available from the British Library.

Microsoft Press books are available through booksellers and distributors worldwide. For further information about international editions, contact your local Microsoft Corporation office or contact Microsoft Press International directly at fax (425) 936-7329. Visit our Web site at www.microsoft.com/mspress. Send comments to *tkinput@microsoft.com*.

**For Microsoft Press**
**Acquisitions Editor:** Kathy Harding
**Project Editor:** Julie Miller

**Author:** Alan R. Carter

**For IQUAD Solutions**
**Project Manager:** Ila Neeley
**Copy Editor:** Merianne Marble
**Technical Editor:** Rich Hillyard
**Desktop Publisher:** Cathy Gilmore

SubAssy Part No. X09-13144
Body Part No. X08-83248

# Introduction

This Lab Manual supplements the *ALS: Managing a Microsoft Windows 2000 Network Environment* textbook. The labs in this manual are designed to be performed in a classroom environment by a group of students under the supervision of an instructor. The approach to these labs differs from the hands-on exercises in the textbook, which are designed to be performed outside the classroom. The labs in this manual and in the hands-on exercises in the textbook are an essential part of your training. The opportunity to explore the menus and dialog boxes in the Windows 2000 user interface will help to ensure your ability to use the many features of Windows 2000.

The labs are performed in a classroom that is set up as an isolated network. The instructor computer is a Microsoft Windows 2000 domain controller named Instructor*x* (where *x* is the number specifically assigned to your instructor's computer). The instructor computer includes shared folders that contain programs and data files that support the labs. Each student computer runs Microsoft Windows 2000 Advanced Server and is configured as a member of Domain*y* (where *y* is a number specifically assigned to your classroom domain).

The Microsoft Certified Professional (MCP) exams are demanding in both the knowledge and the hands-on experience they require. Students preparing for the Microsoft certification tests can increase their competence by gaining first-hand experience in the implementation and management of Windows 2000. One of the best ways to become confident in the use of Windows 2000 Server is to complete all the assigned labs in this manual, as well as the hands-on exercises in the textbook.

# Contents

# Lab 1: Installing and Configuring Networking Components and Using the MMC

## Objectives

After completing this lab, you will be able to

- Install network clients, services, and protocols
- Configure network bindings
- Create and save a customized Microsoft Management Console (MMC)
- Use a customized MMC console to manage a remote computer

**Note** Completing this lab will help reinforce your learning from Chapter 1 of the textbook.

## Before You Begin

You will need to get the following information from your instructor before you begin this lab:

- The number assigned to your instructor's computer: $x$
- The number assigned to your classroom domain: $y$
- Your student number: $z$

**Estimated time to complete the lab: 45 minutes**

# Exercise 1
# Installing Networking Components

In this exercise, you will install the NetBIOS Extended User Interface (NetBEUI) protocol on a computer running Microsoft Windows 2000 Advanced Server.

▶ **To install the NetBEUI protocol**

1. Log on to Domain*y* (where *y* is the domain number) from your student computer as Student*z* (where *z* is your student number), using a password of **M@n2000Net**.

**Note** During the logon process, you will be notified that your password has expired and must be changed. When you change your password, consider using a complex password. Microsoft recommends mixing uppercase and lowercase letters, numbers, and symbols (for example Lp6*g9F2).

2. From the desktop, right-click My Network Places, and then click Properties.
3. In the Network And Dial-Up Connections window, right-click Local Area Connection, and then click Properties.
4. In the Local Area Connection Properties dialog box, click Install.
5. In the Select Network Component Type dialog box, click Client, and then click Add.

   Which network clients are available to install in the Select Network Client dialog box?

   _____

   _____

   _____

   _____

6. In the Select Network Client dialog box, click Cancel.

7. In the Select Network Component Type dialog box, click Service, and then click Add.

   Which network services are available to install in the Select Network Service dialog box?

   _____

   _____

   _____

   _____

8. In the Select Network Service dialog box, click Cancel.

9. In the Select Network Component Type dialog box, click Protocol, and then click Add.

   Which network protocols are available to install in the Select Network Protocol dialog box?

   _____

   _____

   _____

   _____

10. In the Select Network Protocol dialog box, click NetBEUI Protocol, and then click OK.

11. In the Local Area Connection Properties dialog box, click Close.

12. Close the Network And Dial-Up Connections window.

You have successfully installed the NetBEUI protocol.

# Exercise 2
# Configuring Bindings

In this exercise, you will unbind the NetBEUI protocol from a network connection.

▶ **To unbind the NetBEUI protocol**

1. From the desktop, right-click My Network Places, and then click Properties.

2. In the Network And Dial-Up Connections window, right-click Local Area Connection, and then click Properties.

3. In the Local Area Connection Properties dialog box, in the Components Checked Are Used By This Connection box, clear the check box next to NetBEUI Protocol, and then click OK.

---

**Tip** To rebind the NetBEUI protocol to this connection in the future, simply repeat this procedure and select the check box next to NetBEUI Protocol instead of clearing it.

---

4. Close the Network And Dial-Up Connections window.

You have successfully unbound the NetBEUI protocol from the network connection named Local Area Connection.

# Exercise 3
# Creating and Saving a Customized MMC Console

In this exercise, you will create and save a customized MMC console.

▶ **To create and save a customized MMC console**

1. From the desktop, click Start, and then click Run.

2. In the Run dialog box, in the Open text box, type **mmc** and then click OK.

3. In the Console1 window, expand the Console Root window by clicking the maximize button in the upper right corner of the window, and then maximize the Console1 – [Console Root] window.

4. On the Console menu, click Add/Remove Snap-In.

5. In the Add/Remove Snap-In dialog box, click Add.

6. In the Add Standalone Snap-In dialog box, click Active Directory Users And Computers, and then click Add.

7. Click Computer Management, and then click Add.

8. In the Computer Management dialog box, select Local Computer, and then click Finish.

9. In the Add Standalone Snap-In dialog box, click Routing And Remote Access, and then click Add.

10. Click Close.

11. In the Add/Remove Snap-In dialog box, click OK.

12. In the Console1 – [Console Root] window, right-click the Console Root folder, and then click Rename.

13. Type **My Custom MMC** and then press ENTER.

14. On the Console menu, click Options.

    Which options are available in the Console Mode drop-down list box?

    _____

    _____

    _____

    _____

15. In the Options dialog box, from the Console Mode drop-down list box, select User Mode – Full Access, and then click OK.

16. On the Console menu, click Save As.

17. In the Save As dialog box, in the File Name box, type **MyCustomMMC** and then click Save.

18. Close the MyCustomMMC window.

19. In the Microsoft Management Console dialog box, click Yes.

20. Click Start, point to Programs, and then point to Administrative Tools.

    Notice that MyCustomMMC is now one of your administrative tools.

21. To close the Start menu, click the desktop.

You have created and saved a customized MMC console named MyCustomMMC.

# Exercise 4
# Managing a Remote Computer by Using a Customized MMC Console

In this exercise, you will use your customized MMC console to manage the instructor's computer.

▶ **To manage a remote computer**

1. From the desktop, click Start, point to Programs, point to Administrative Tools, and then click MyCustomMMC.

2. In the left pane of the MyCustomMMC window, click Computer Management (Local), then right-click Computer Management (Local), and then click the Connect To Another Computer menu option.

3. In the Select Computer dialog box, double-click Instructor*x* (where *x* is the number of your instructor's computer).

    Notice that Computer Management (Local) has changed to Computer Management (Instructor*x*.Domain*y*.com) (where *x* is the number of your instructor's computer, and *y* is the number assigned to your classroom's domain).

4. In the left pane of the MyCustomMMC window, expand Computer Management (Instructor*x*.Domain*y*.com), expand System Tools, and then expand Shared Folders.

5. In the left pane of the MyCustomMMC window, click Shares.

    Which shared folders are available on the instructor's computer?

    _____

    _____

    _____

6. In the right pane of the MyCustomMMC window, right-click the W2000Srv shared folder, and then click the Properties menu option.

7. In the W2000Srv Properties dialog box, click the Share Permissions tab.

---

**Caution**  Do not change any of the permissions assigned to this shared folder. If you do, you might cause problems for other students, and you could also cause problems with other lab exercises.

---

Which permissions are assigned to the W2000Srv shared folder?

_____

_____

8. In the W2000Srv Properties dialog box, click Cancel.

9. In the left pane of the MyCustomMMC window, click the Sessions folder.

   Note which users are connected to the instructor's computer and which computer they are connected from.

10. In the left pane of the MyCustomMMC window, click Computer Management (Instructor*x*.Domain*y*.com), right-click Computer Management (Instructor*x*.Domain*y*.com), and then click the Connect To Another Computer menu option.

11. In the Select Computer dialog box, double-click your computer name.

   The left pane should now include Computer Management (Local).

**Note** If you do not reconnect Computer Management to your local computer, the next time you open your customized MMC console, Computer Management will still be focused on the instructor's computer.

12. Close the MyCustomMMC window.

You have used your customized MMC console to connect to and manage a remote computer.

# Lab 2: Configuring and Managing Driver Signing, Updates, Licensing, and System Recovery

## Objectives

After completing this lab, you will be able to

- Configure and verify driver signing
- Install a service pack
- Install the Recovery Console
- Create and view a boot log file

---

**Note** Completing this lab will help reinforce your learning from Chapter 2 of the textbook.

---

## Before You Begin

This lab is dependent on Lab 1. You must have completed Lab 1 before you begin this lab.

You will need to get the following information from your instructor before you begin this lab:

- The number assigned to your instructor's computer: $x$
- The number assigned to your classroom domain: $y$
- Your student number: $z$

You will also need the *Microsoft Windows 2000 Advanced Server* CD-ROM that came with your textbook for the class.

**Estimated time to complete the lab: 45 minutes**

# Exercise 1
# Configuring and Verifying Driver Signing

In this exercise, you will configure driver signing options and then use Sigverif.exe to verify driver signing on your student computer.

▶ **To configure and verify driver signing**

1. Log on to Domain*y* (where *y* is the domain number) from your student computer as Student*z* (where *z* is your student number), using the password you established in Lab 1.

2. From the desktop, right-click My Computer, and then click Properties.

3. In the System Properties dialog box, click the Hardware tab.

4. Click Driver Signing.

5. In the Driver Signing Options dialog box, click the Block – Prevent Installation Of Unsigned Files option, and then click OK.

   This will prevent the installation of any driver files that have not passed the Microsoft certification process and do not have a digital signature from Microsoft on them.

6. In the System Properties dialog box, click OK.

7. From the desktop, click Start, and then click Run.

8. In the Run dialog box, in the Open box, type **sigverif** and then click OK.

9. In the File Signature Verification dialog box, click Start.

10. If a SigVerif dialog box appears, indicating that your files have been scanned and verified, click OK.

    If a Signature Verification Results dialog box appears, review the list of files on your computer that have not been digitally signed, and then click Close.

11. In the File Signature Verification dialog box, click Close.

You have successfully configured driver signing options and used Sigverif.exe to determine whether all of your system files have valid digital signatures.

# Exercise 2
# Installing a Service Pack

In this exercise, you will install Microsoft Windows 2000 Server Pack 2 (SP2) on your student computer.

▶   **To install Service Pack 2**

1. From the desktop, click Start, and then click Run.

2. In the Run dialog box, in the Open box, type
   **\\Instructor.x\LabFiles\Sp2\W2ksp2\** (where *x* is the number of your instructor's computer), and then click OK.

   An Extracting Files message box appears, indicating that the service pack files are being extracted. This may take a couple of minutes to complete.

3. When the Windows 2000 Service Pack Setup dialog appears, click the check box next to Accept The License Agreement.

   Notice that the check box next to Backup Files Necessary To Uninstall This Service Pack At A Later Time is selected by default. If you clear this check box, you will not be able to uninstall the service pack.

4. Click Install.

   Windows 2000 backs up the necessary files to enable you to uninstall the service pack at a later time, and then installs the service pack. This process will take several minutes to complete.

5. When the Windows 2000 Service Pack Setup message box indicates that the installation is complete, click Restart to restart your computer.

You have successfully installed Service Pack 2 on your computer.

# Exercise 3
# Installing the Recovery Console

In this exercise, you will install the Recovery Console as a Boot menu option.

▶ **To install the Recovery Console**

1. Insert the *Microsoft Windows 2000 Advanced Server* CD-ROM into the CD-ROM drive.

2. If a Microsoft Windows 2000 CD dialog box appears, click Exit.

3. From the desktop, click Start, and then click Run.

4. In the Run dialog box, in the Open box, type *d*:**\I386\Winnt32 /cmdcons** (where *d* is the drive letter of the CD-ROM drive on your computer), and then click OK.

5. In the Windows 2000 Setup dialog box, click Yes to install the Recovery Console.

   After the Recovery Console is installed, a Microsoft Windows 2000 Advanced Server Setup message box indicates that the Recovery Console has been successfully installed.

6. In the Microsoft Windows 2000 Advanced Server Setup message box, click OK.

You have successfully installed the Recovery Console on your computer. It will now appear as an option on the Boot menu.

# Exercise 4
# Creating and Viewing a Boot Log File

In this exercise, you will reboot your computer and then enable boot logging. Finally, you will view the boot log file in Microsoft Notepad.

▶ **To create and view a boot log file**

1. Click Start, and then click Shut Down.

2. In the Shut Down Windows dialog box, select Restart from the What Do You Want The Computer To Do? box, and then click OK.

   Microsoft Windows 2000 Advanced Server shuts down and then begins the restart process.

3. In the Please Select An Operating System To Start menu, press F8 to access the advanced startup options.

4. In the Windows 2000 Advanced Options menu, select Enable Boot Logging, and then press ENTER.

5. In the Please Select An Operating System To Start menu, select Microsoft Windows 2000 Advanced Server, and then press ENTER.

6. Log on to Domain$y$ (where $y$ is the domain number) from your student computer as Student$z$ (where $z$ is your student number), using the password you established in Lab 1.

7. From the desktop, click Start, and then click Run.

8. In the Run dialog box, in the Open box, type **C:\Winnt\Ntbtlog.txt** and then click OK.

9. In the Ntbtlog – Notepad window, view the contents of the boot log file you created.

   Notice that the service pack level, date, and time are listed at the beginning of the boot log file. Also notice that a complete list of the drivers that were loaded, and the drivers that were not loaded, is included in the file. This file can be used to troubleshoot boot problems on computers running Windows 2000.

10. Close Notepad.

You have successfully created and viewed a boot log file on your computer.

# Lab 3: Managing Disks

## Objectives

After completing this lab, you will be able to

- Convert a basic disk to a dynamic disk
- Create a simple volume
- Configure disk quotas

---

**Note** Completing this lab will help reinforce your learning from Chapter 3 of the textbook.

---

## Before You Begin

This lab is dependent on Lab 1. You must have completed Lab 1 before you begin this lab.

You will need to get the following information from your instructor before you begin this lab:

- The number assigned to your classroom domain: $y$
- Your student number: $z$

**Estimated time to complete the lab: 30 minutes**

# Exercise 1
# Converting a Basic Disk to a Dynamic Disk

In this exercise, you will convert the disk in your student computer from a basic disk to a dynamic disk.

▶   **To convert a basic disk to a dynamic disk**

1. Log on to Domain*y* (where *y* is the domain number) from your student computer as Student*z* (where *z* is your student number), using the password you established in Lab 1.

2. From the desktop, click Start, point to Programs, point to Administrative Tools, and then click MyCustomMMC.

3. In the left pane of the MyCustomMMC window, expand Computer Management (Local), expand Storage, and then click Disk Management.

4. In the right pane, right-click Disk 0, and then click Upgrade To Dynamic Disk.

5. In the Upgrade To Dynamic Disk dialog box, ensure that the check box next to Disk 0 is selected, and then click OK.

6. In the Disks To Upgrade dialog box, click Upgrade.

7. In the Disk Management dialog box, click Yes.

8. In the Upgrade Disks dialog box, click Yes.

9. In the Confirm message box, click OK to reboot your computer and complete the process of upgrading your disk to a dynamic disk.

10. Log on to Domain*y* from your student computer as Student*z*.

11. In the System Settings Change message box, click Yes to reboot your computer again.

---

**Note** This second reboot is required because the dynamic disk appears as a new hardware device to the operating system, and a reboot is required to finish the installation of the dynamic disk.

---

You have successfully converted your disk to a dynamic disk.

# Exercise 2
# Creating a Simple Volume

In this exercise, you will use the Disk Management snap-in to create a simple volume on your computer.

▶ **To create a simple volume**

1. Log on to Domain*y* (where *y* is the domain number) from your student computer as Student*z* (where *z* is your student number), using the password you established in Lab 1.

2. From the desktop, click Start, point to Programs, point to Administrative Tools, and then click MyCustomMMC.

3. In the left pane of the MyCustomMMC window, expand Computer Management (Local), expand Storage, and then click Disk Management.

   Notice that your disk has been upgraded to a dynamic disk.

4. In the right pane, right-click the area of unallocated space on Disk 0, and then click Create Volume.

   The Create Volume Wizard starts.

5. On the Create Volume Wizard page, click Next.

6. On the Select Volume Type page, select Simple Volume, and then click Next.

   The Select Disks page appears, with Disk 0 listed under Selected Dynamic Disks.

7. On the Select Disks page, click Next.

8. On the Assign Drive Letter Or Path page, click Next to accept the default drive letter assignment.

9. On the Format Volume page, ensure that the Format This Volume As Follows option is selected, and ensure that NTFS is selected in the File System To Use drop-down list.

10. In the Volume Label text box, delete the existing volume label text, type **SimpleVol** and then click Next.

11. On the Completing The Create Volume Wizard page, click Finish to create and format the new volume.

You have successfully created a simple volume.

# Exercise 3
# Configuring Encryption

In this exercise, you will configure file encryption and then log on as a different user to see the results of encryption.

▶    **To configure encryption**

1. Log on to Domain*y* (where *y* is the domain number) from your student computer as User*z* (where *z* is your student number), using a password of **M@n2000Net**.

---

**Note** During the logon process, you will be notified that your password has expired and must be changed. When you change your password, consider using a complex password. Microsoft recommends mixing uppercase and lowercase letters, numbers, and symbols (for example, Lp6*g9F2).

---

2. From the desktop, right-click My Computer, and then click Explore.

3. In the left pane of the My Computer window, click Local Disk (C:).

4. On the File menu, point to New, and then click Text Document.

5. In the right pane, type **Encrypted.txt** as the file name.

6. Double-click the file named Encrypted.txt.

7. In the Encrypted.txt Microsoft Notepad window, type **This file is an encrypted file**.

8. On the File menu, click Exit.

9. In the Notepad dialog box, click Yes to save the changes you made to the text file.

10. In the right pane of the Local Disk (C:) window, right-click the Encrypted.txt file, and then click Properties.

11. In the Encrypted.txt Properties dialog box, click Advanced.

12. In the Advanced Attributes dialog box, in the General tab, select the Encrypt Contents To Secure Data check box, and then click OK.

13. In the Encrypted.txt Properties dialog box, click OK.

    You have now successfully encrypted the Encrypted.txt file.

14. In the right pane of the Local Disk (C:) window, double-click the file named Encrypted.txt.

    Can you open the file? Why or why not?

    _____

    _____

15. Close Windows Explorer.

16. Click Start, and then click Shut Down.

17. In the Shut Down Windows dialog box, in the What Do You Want The Computer To Do? box, select the Log Off User*z* option, and then click OK.

18. Log on to Domain*y* from your student computer as Student*z*, using the password you established in Lab 1.

19. From the desktop, right-click My Computer, and then click Explore.

20. In the left pane of the My Computer window, click Local Disk (C:).

21. In the right pane, right-click the Encrypted.txt file, and then click Properties.

22. In the Encrypted.txt Properties dialog box, click the Security tab.

    Which permissions are assigned to the Encrypted.txt file?

    _____

    _____

23. In the Encrypted.txt Properties dialog box, click Cancel.

24. In the right pane, double-click the Encrypted.txt file.

    Can you open the file? Why or why not?

    _____

    _____

25. Close Notepad.

26. Close Windows Explorer.

You have successfully configured encryption for a file and then logged on as a different user

# Lab 4:  Managing NTFS Permissions

## Objectives

After completing this lab, you will be able to

- Modify NT file system (NTFS) permissions for a volume
- Assign standard NTFS permissions
- Assign special NTFS permissions and take ownership of a folder

**Note**  Completing this lab will help reinforce your learning from Chapter 4 of the textbook.

## Before You Begin

You will need to get the following information from your instructor before you begin this lab:

- The number assigned to your classroom domain: $y$
- Your student number: $z$

**Estimated time to complete the lab: 40 minutes**

# Exercise 1
# Modifying the NTFS Permissions for a Volume

In this exercise, you will modify the NTFS permissions that are assigned to the root of a volume.

▶   **To modify permissions for a volume**

1. Log on to Domain*y* (where *y* is the domain number) from your student computer as Student*z* (where *z* is your student number).

2. From the desktop, right-click My Computer, and then click Explore.

3. In the left pane of the My Computer window, right-click Local Disk (C:), and then click Properties.

4. In the Local Disk (C:) Properties dialog box, click the Security tab.

5. In the Security tab, click Add.

6. In the Select Users, Computers, Or Groups dialog box, in the Name list, select the System group, and then click Add.

7. Select the Domain Admins group, and then click Add.

8. Click OK.

9. In the Local Disk (C:) Properties dialog box, in the Name list, select Domain Admins, and then in the Permissions list, select the Allow check box next to Full Control.

10. In the Name list, select the System group, and then in the Permissions list, select the Allow check box next to Full Control.

11. In the Name list, select the Everyone group, and then in the Permissions list, ensure that only the Allow check box next to List Folder Contents is selected and that all other Allow check boxes are cleared.

12. Click OK.

13. Close Windows Explorer.

You have successfully modified the default permissions for drive C.

# Exercise 2
# Assigning Standard NTFS Permissions

In this exercise, you will create the SharedData folder and assign NTFS permissions to the folder.

▶  **To assign standard NTFS permissions**

1. Log on to Domain*y* (where *y* is the domain number) from your student computer as Student*z* (where *z* is your student number).

2. From the desktop, right-click My Computer, and then click Explore.

3. In the left pane of the My Computer window, click Local Disk (C:).

4. On the File menu, point to New, and then click Folder.

5. Name the new folder **SharedData**.

6. In the right pane of the My Computer window, right-click the SharedData folder, and then click Properties.

7. In the SharedData Properties dialog box, click the Security tab.

   Notice that the SharedData folder has inherited the permissions you assigned to the root of drive C in Exercise 1.

8. Clear the Allow Inheritable Permissions From Parent To Propagate To This Object check box.

9. In the Security dialog box, click Remove.

10. In the SharedData Properties dialog box, click Add.

11. In the Select Users, Computers, Or Groups dialog box, in the Name list, select the Creator Owner group, and then click Add.

12. Select the Everyone group, and then click Add.

13. Click OK.

14. In the SharedData Properties dialog box, in the Name list, select Creator Owner, and then in the Permissions list, select the Allow check box next to Full Control.

15. In the Name list, select Everyone, and then in the Permissions list, select the Allow check box next to Write, then ensure that the Allow check boxes next to List Folder Contents and Read are already selected, and then click OK.

16. Close Windows Explorer.

17. Log off as Student*z*, and then log on to your computer as User*z* (where *z* is your student number), using the password you established in Lab 3.

18. From the desktop, right-click My Computer, and then click Explore.

19. In the left pane of the My Computer window, click Local Disk (C:).

20. In the right pane of the Local Disk (C:) window, double-click the SharedData folder.

21. On the File menu, point to New, and then click Text Document.

22. Name the new file **User.txt**.

23. In the right pane, right-click the User.txt file, and then click Properties.

24. In the User.txt Properties dialog box, click the Security tab.

    What permissions are assigned to the Userz user account for the User.txt file? Why?

    _____

    _____

    _____

    _____

25. Close Windows Explorer.

You have created a new folder and assigned permissions for various groups to the new folder. You have also tested the permissions you assigned to the folder by logging on as a different user and creating a new text file in the folder.

# Exercise 3
# Assigning Special NTFS Permissions and Taking Ownership of a Folder

In this exercise, you will assign special NTFS permissions to a folder and then log on as a different user and take ownership of that folder.

▶ **To assign special NTFS permissions and take ownership of a folder**

1. Log on to Domain*y* (where *y* is the domain number) from your student computer as Student*z* (where *z* is your student number).

2. From the desktop, right-click My Computer, and then click Explore.

3. In the left pane of the My Computer window, click Local Disk (C:).

4. On the File menu, point to New, and then click Folder.

5. Name the new folder **NewOwner**.

6. In the right pane of the My Computer window, right-click the NewOwner folder, and then click Properties.

7. In the NewOwner Properties dialog box, click the Security tab.

8. In the Security tab, click Add.

9. In the Select Users, Computers, Or Groups dialog box, in the Name list, select the user named User*z*, and then click Add.

10. Click OK.

11. In the NewOwner Properties dialog box, click Advanced.

12. In the Access Control Settings For NewOwner dialog box, in the Permission Entries box, double-click the entry for User*z*.

13. In the Permission Entry For NewOwner dialog box, select the Allow check box next to Take Ownership, and then click OK.

14. In the Access Control Settings For NewOwner dialog box, click OK.

15. In the NewOwner Properties dialog box, click OK.

16. Close Windows Explorer.

17. Log off as Student*z*, and then log on to your computer as User*z*, using the password you established in Lab 3.

18. From the desktop, right-click My Computer, and then click Explore.

19. In the left pane of the My Computer window, click Local Disk (C:).

20. In the right pane of the Local Disk (C:) window, right-click the NewOwner folder, and then click Properties.

21. In the NewOwner Properties dialog box, click the Security tab.

22. In the Security message box, click OK.

23. In the NewOwner Properties dialog box, click Advanced.

24. In the Access Control Settings For NewOwner dialog box, click the Owner tab. Who is the current owner of the NewOwner folder?

_____

25. In the Change Owner To box, select your user name, and then click OK.

26. In the NewOwner Properties dialog box, click OK.

27. Close Windows Explorer.

You have successfully assigned special permissions to a folder and then logged on as a different user and taken ownership of that folder.

# Lab 5: Managing Shared Resources

## Objectives

After completing this lab, you will be able to

- Configure shared folders and shared folder permissions
- Create a distributed file system (Dfs) root and Dfs links
- Install, configure, share, and manage printers

---

**Note** Completing this lab will help reinforce your learning from Chapter 5 of the textbook.

---

## Before You Begin

You will need to get the following information from your instructor before you begin this lab:

- The number assigned to your instructor's computer: $x$
- The number assigned to your classroom domain: $y$
- Your student number: $z$

You will also need the *Microsoft Windows 2000 Advanced Server* CD-ROM that came with your textbook for the class.

**Estimated time to complete the lab: 1 hour 20 minutes**

# Exercise 1
# Configuring a Shared Folder and Shared Folder Permissions

In this exercise, you will share a folder and assign shared folder permissions to the shared folder.

▶ **To configure a shared folder and shared folder permissions**

1. Log on to Domain*y* (where *y* is the domain number) from your student computer as Student*z* (where *z* is your student number).
2. From the desktop, right-click My Computer, and then click Explore.
3. In the left pane of the My Computer window, right-click Local Disk (C:).
4. In the right pane, right-click the SharedData folder, and then click Properties.
5. In the SharedData Properties dialog box, click the Sharing tab.
6. In the Sharing tab, select Share This Folder, and then click Permissions.
7. In the Permissions For SharedData dialog box, in the Name list, select Everyone, and then clear the Allow check box next to Full Control.
8. Click Add.
9. In the Select Users, Computers, Or Groups dialog box, select the Student*z* user account, and then click Add.
10. Click OK to close the Select Users, Computers, Or Groups dialog box.
11. In the Permissions for SharedData dialog box, in the Name list, select Student*z*, and then select the Allow check box next to Full Control.
12. Click OK.
13. In the SharedData Properties dialog box, click OK.
14. Close Windows Explorer.

You have successfully shared a folder and configured share permissions for the shared folder.

# Exercise 2
# Creating a Dfs Root and Dfs Links

In this exercise, you will create a Dfs root and several Dfs links.

▶ **To create a Dfs root and Dfs links**

1. Log on to Domain*y* (where *y* is the domain number) from your student computer as Student*z* (where *z* is your student number).

2. From the desktop, click Start, point to Programs, point to Administrative Tools, and then click Distributed File System.

3. In the Distributed File System window, click the Action menu, and then click New Dfs Root.

4. On the Welcome To The New Dfs Root Wizard page, click Next.

5. On the Select The Dfs Root Type page, select Create A Standalone Dfs Root, and then click Next.

6. On the Specify The Host Server For The Dfs Root page, ensure that your server name appears in the Server Name box, and then click Next.

7. On the Specify The Dfs Root Share page, select Create A New Share.

8. In the Path To Share box, type **C:\Dfs**.

9. In the Share Name box, type **MyDfs** and then click Next.

10. In the Distributed File System message box, click Yes to create the C:\Dfs folder.

11. On the Name The Dfs Root page, in the Comment box, type **My Dfs Share** and then click Next.

12. On the Completing The New Dfs Root Wizard page, click Finish.

    The Dfs root you just created appears in the Distributed File System window.

13. In the Distributed File System window, in the left pane, click the Dfs root you just created.

14. From the Action menu, click New Dfs Link.

15. In the Create A New Dfs Link dialog box, in the Link Name box, type **SharedData**.

16. In the Send The User To This Shared Folder box, type **\\Serverz\SharedData** and then click OK.

17. In the left pane of the Distributed File System window, right-click your computer's Dfs root (not the Dfs link you just created), and then click New Dfs Link.

18. In the Create A New Dfs Link dialog box, in the Link Name box, type **LabFiles**.

19. In the Send The User To This Shared Folder box, type
    **\\Instructor***x***\LabFiles** (where *x* is the number of your instructor's
    computer), and then click OK.

20. In the left pane of the Distributed File System window, right-click your
    computer's Dfs root, and then click New Dfs Link.

21. In the Create A New Dfs Link dialog box, in the Link Name box, type
    **W2000Srv**.

22. In the Send The User To This Shared Folder box, type
    **\\Instructor***x***\W2000Srv** and then click OK.

23. Close the Distributed File System window.

24. From the desktop, right-click My Computer, and then click Explore.

25. In the My Computer window, click the Tools menu, and then click Map
    Network Drive.

26. In the Map Network Drive dialog box, in the Folder box, type
    **\\Server***z***\MyDfs** and then click Finish.

    Which subfolders are displayed in the MyDfs On 'Server*z*' dialog box?

    _____

    _____

    What happens when you double-click the W2000Srv folder?

    _____

    _____

27. Close Windows Explorer.

You have successfully created a Dfs root and three Dfs links. You have also
mapped a network drive to the Dfs root and viewed its contents.

# Exercise 3
# Installing, Configuring, Sharing, and Managing Printers

In this exercise, you will install, configure, share, and manage a printer.

**Note** No physical print device is required to perform this exercise.

▶ **To install and share a printer**

1. Log on to Domain*y* (where *y* is the domain number) from your student computer as Student*z* (where *z* is your student number).
2. From the desktop, click Start, point to Settings, and then click Printers.
3. In the Printers dialog box, double-click Add Printer.

   The Add Printer Wizard starts.
4. On the Welcome To The Add Printer Wizard page, click Next.
5. On the Local Or Network Printer page, click Local Printer, and then clear the Automatically Detect And Install My Plug And Play Printer check box.
6. Click Next.
7. On the Select The Printer Port page, ensure that the Use The Following Port option is selected and that LPT1: is selected in the Port list.
8. Click Next.
9. On the Add Printer Wizard page, in the Manufacturers list, select HP; in the Printers list, select HP LaserJet 4.
10. Click Next.
11. On the Name Your Printer page, accept the default name of HP LaserJet 4, and then click Next.
12. On the Printer Sharing page, select Share As, accept the default share name of HPLaserJ, and then click Next .
13. On the Location And Comment page, in the Location box, type **On my computer** and then click Next.
14. On the Print Test Page page, select No, and then click Next.
15. On the Completing The Add Printer Wizard page, click Finish.

    Windows 2000 copies the files needed for the new printer and then closes the Add Printer Wizard.

You have successfully installed and shared a printer on your computer.

In the next procedure, you will configure the printer you just installed by installing drivers for an additional operating system and specifying a separator page.

► **To configure a printer**

1. In the Printers dialog box, right-click HP LaserJet 4, and then click Use Printer Offline.

2. In the Printers dialog box, right-click HP LaserJet 4, and then click Properties.

3. In the HP LaserJet 4 Properties dialog box, click the Sharing tab.

4. In the Sharing tab, click Additional Drivers.

5. In the Additional Drivers dialog box, select the check box on the line for the Windows NT 4.0 Or 2000 option, and then click OK.

   The Insert Disk dialog box appears, prompting you to insert your Windows 2000 Server CD-ROM. Insert your Windows 2000 Advanced Server CD-ROM into your computer's CD-ROM drive.

6. Close the Microsoft Windows 2000 CD dialog box.

7. In the Insert Disk dialog box, click OK.

   Windows 2000 copies the files needed.

8. In the HP LaserJet 4 Properties dialog box, click the Advanced tab.

9. In the Advanced tab, click Separator Page.

10. In the Separator Page dialog box, click Browse.

11. In the Separator Page list, double-click Pcl.sep, and then in the Separator Page dialog box, click OK.

12. In the HP LaserJet 4 Properties dialog box, click Close.

13. Close the Printers dialog box.

You have successfully installed drivers for an additional operating system, and configured a separator page for the printer.

In the next procedure, you will use Microsoft Internet Explorer to manage the printer.

► **To manage a printer**

1. From the desktop, double-click Internet Explorer.

**Note** An Internet connection is not required to perform this exercise.

2. On the Welcome To The Internet Connection Wizard page, select I Want To Set Up My Internet Connection Manually, and then click Next.

3. On the Setting Up Your Internet Connection page, select I Connect Through A Local Area Network, and then click Next.

4. On the Local Area Network Internet Configuration page, clear the Automatic Discovery Of Proxy Server check box, and then click Next.

5. On the Set Up Your Internet Mail Account page, select No, and then click Next.

6. On the Completing The Internet Connection Wizard page, click Finish.

7. In the Internet Explorer dialog box, in the Address box, type **http://serverz/printers** (where *z* is your student number), and then press ENTER.

8. From the File menu, click Print.

9. In the Print dialog box, click Print.

   This sends a print job to your printer. The print job will be kept in the printer's print queue because you have configured your printer to use it offline.

10. In the All Printers On Serverz dialog box, in the Name list, click HP LaserJet 4.

11. In the HP LaserJet 4 dialog box, in the Document list, select the All Printers On Serverz document, and then in the Document Actions list in the left pane, click Cancel.

12. Close Internet Explorer and log off the domain.

You have successfully used Internet Explorer to send a document to the printer and have deleted the document by using the Web-based printer management tool.

# Lab 6: Monitoring Your Server

## Objectives

After completing this lab, you will be able to

- Use Windows Task Manager to view processor performance and to stop applications
- Use the Performance console to monitor server performance
- Use the Shared Folders snap-in to monitor connections to a remote computer and to share folders on the remote computer
- Configure an audit policy for an organizational unit (OU) in the Active Directory service and use the security log in Event Viewer to view audit events

---

**Note** Completing this lab will help reinforce your learning from Chapter 6 of the textbook.

---

## Before You Begin

You will need to get the following information from your instructor before you begin this lab:

- The name of your partner's computer (your instructor will assign partners for this lab)
- The number assigned to your classroom domain: $y$
- Your student number: $z$

**Estimated time to complete the lab: 1 hour 15 minutes**

# Exercise 1
# Using Windows Task Manager to View Processor Performance and to Stop Applications

In this exercise, you will use Windows Task Manager to view the performance of the processor in your computer while you play a game of Pinball, and then you will use Task Manager to end the Pinball application.

▶ **To use Windows Task Manager to view processor performance and to stop applications**

1. Log on to Domain*y* (where *y* is the domain number) from your student computer as Student*z* (where *z* is your student number).

2. From the desktop, right-click any blank space on the taskbar, and then click Task Manager.

3. In the Windows Task Manager dialog box, click the Performance tab.

   What is the CPU Usage percentage on your computer right now?

   _____

4. From the desktop, click Start, point to Programs, point to Accessories, point to Games, and then click Pinball.

   What is the CPU Usage percentage on your computer after Pinball is started?

   _____

5. In the Windows Task Manager dialog box, click the Applications tab.

6. In the Applications tab, select 3D Pinball For Windows, and then click End Task.

7. Close Windows Task Manager.

You have successfully used Windows Task Manager to view CPU usage on your computer and to end a program.

# Exercise 2
# Using the Performance Console to Monitor Server Performance

In this exercise, you will use the Performance console to monitor your classroom server's performance.

▶ **To use the Performance console to monitor server performance**

1. From the desktop, click Start, point to Programs, point to Administrative Tools, and then click Performance.

2. In the right pane of the Performance console, right-click the graph area, and then click Add Counters.

3. In the Add Counters dialog box, select Use Local Computer Counters.

4. In the Performance Object box, select Processor, then in the Select Counters From List box, select %Processor Time, then in the Select Instances From List box, click Total, and then click Add.

5. In the Performance Object box, select Memory, then in the Select Counters From List box, select Pages/Sec, and then click Add.

6. In the Performance Object box, select PhysicalDisk, then in the Select Counters From List box, select %Disk Time, then in the Select Instances From List box, click Total, and then click Add.

7. In the Add Counters dialog box, click Close.

8. Watch the graph display for about 30 seconds.

   What is your computer's average for each of the counters?

---

**Tip** To view the average for a counter, select the counter in the list of counters at the bottom of the Performance console, and then read the average in the Average box that is directly above the list of counters.

---

 

 

 

9. Minimize (but do not close) the Performance console window.

10. Right-click the desktop, and then click Properties.

11. In the Display Properties dialog box, click the Screen Saver tab.

12. In the Screen Saver tab, in the Screen Saver list, select 3D Pipes (OpenGL), and then click Preview.

13. Watch the 3D Pipes screen saver for about a minute, and then move the mouse to redisplay the desktop.

14. When the desktop is displayed, quickly maximize the Performance console window.

15. In the Performance console window, click the Freeze Display button (the red button with a white X in its center near the right side of the toolbar) to freeze the display.

What is your computer's average for each of the counters now?

_____

_____

_____

Were there any large spikes in the graph?

_____

_____

_____

Overall, what effect do you think the 3D Pipes screen saver had on the performance of your server?

_____

_____

16. Close the Performance console window.

17. In the Display Properties dialog box, click Cancel.

You have successfully started the Performance console, established a baseline for your server, and then measured the performance of your server under a load. (The load was the 3D Pipes screen saver.)

# Exercise 3
# Using the Shared Folders Tool to Monitor Connections to Your Partner's Computer and to Share a Folder on Your Partner's Computer

In this exercise, you will use the Shared Folders tool to monitor connections to your partner's computer and then share a folder on your partner's computer.

**Note** Your instructor will assign partners for this lab. Write down your partner's computer name here before you start this exercise.

---

►    **To use the Shared Folders tool to monitor connections on your partner's computer and to share a folder on your partner's computer**

1. From the desktop, right-click My Computer, and then click Manage.

2. In the Computer Management window, in the left pane, right-click Computer Management (Local), and then click Connect To Another Computer.

3. In the Select Computer dialog box, double-click your partner's computer name.

4. In the Computer Management window, in the left pane, expand System Tools, and then expand Shared Folders.

5. In the left pane, select the Shares folder.

   Which shares are available on your partner's computer?

   _____

   _____

6. In the left pane, select the Sessions folder.

   Which sessions are listed on your partner's computer?

   _____

   _____

7. In the left pane, select the Open Files folder.

Which open files are listed on your partner's computer?

_____

_____

8. In the left pane, select the Shares folder.

9. From the Action menu, click New File Share.

10. In the Create Shared Folder dialog box, in the Folder To Share text box, type **C:\SharedData**.

11. In the Share Name text box, type **Data$** and then click Next.

12. In the next Create Shared Folder dialog box, select Administrators Have Full Control; Other Users Have No Access, and then click Finish.

13. In the next Create Shared Folder dialog box, click No.

14. Close the Computer Management window.

You have successfully used the Shared Folders tool to view shares, sessions, and open files on your partner's computer. You have also created a new hidden shared folder named Data$ on your partner's computer.

# Exercise 4
# Configuring an Audit Policy for an OU in Active Directory, and Using the Security Log in Event Viewer to View Audit Events

In this exercise, you will configure an audit policy for an OU in Active Directory and then use the security log in Event Viewer to view audit events.

▶ **To configure an audit policy for an OU in Active Directory**

**Note**  To complete this exercise, you must be logged on to Domain*y* (where *y* is the domain number) from your student computer as Student*z* (where *z* is your student number).

1. From the desktop, click Start, point to Programs, point to Administrative Tools, and then click MyCustomMMC.
2. In the left pane of the MyCustomMMC console, expand Active Directory Users And Computers, and then expand Domain*y*.com.
3. In the left pane, select the Computers container.
4. In the right pane, right-click Server*z*, and then click Move.
5. In the Move dialog box, click OU*z*, and then click OK.
6. In the left pane, click OU*z*.

   Which Active Directory objects are displayed in the right pane?

   _____

   _____

7. In the left pane, right-click OU*z*, and then click Properties.
8. In the OU*z* Properties dialog box, click the Group Policy tab.
9. In the Group Policy tab, click New, and then for the new Group Policy Object name, type **Auditing**.
10. Click Edit.
11. In the Group Policy window, in the left pane, expand the Windows Settings folder that appears underneath Computer Configuration, then expand Security Settings, and then expand Local Policies.
12. Select Audit Policy.
13. In the right pane, double-click Audit Account Logon Events.

14. In the Security Policy Setting dialog box, select the Define These Policy Settings check box, then select the check boxes next to Success and Failure, and then click OK.

15. Close the Group Policy window.

16. In the OU*z* Properties dialog box, click Close.

17. Close the MyCustomMMC console.

18. Shut down and then restart your computer.

    Restarting your computer will cause all of the group policy settings you just configured to take effect.

19. Attempt to log on to your student computer (not to the domain) as User*z*, using a password of **wrongpassword**.

    This will create a security audit event for a failed logon attempt.

20. Attempt to log on to your student computer (not to the domain) as Student*z*, using a password of **wrongpassword**.

    This will create an additional security audit event.

You have successfully configured an audit policy that audits success and failure logon events, and then you have created two failure logon events by attempting to log on to your computer using an incorrect username and password.

► **To use the security log in Event Viewer to view audit events**

1. Log on to Domain*y* (where *y* is the domain number) from your student computer as Student*z*, (where *z* is your student number), using your correct password.

2. From the desktop, click Start, point to Programs, point to Administrative Tools, and then click MyCustomMMC.

3. In the left pane of the MyCustomMMC window, expand Computer Management (Local), expand System Tools, expand Event Viewer, and then click Security.

   What is displayed in the right pane of the MyCustomMMC window?

   _____

   _____

4. Close the MyCustomMMC console.

You have successfully viewed the auditing results in Event Viewer.

# Lab 7: Managing User Accounts

## Objectives

After completing this lab, you will be able to

- Create local user accounts
- Create and modify domain user accounts
- Maintain domain user accounts
- Configure roaming user profiles

**Note** Completing this lab will help reinforce your learning from Chapter 7 of the textbook.

## Before You Begin

This lab is dependent on Lab 1 and Lab 4. Lab 1 and Lab 4 must be completed before you begin this lab.

You will need to get the following information from your instructor before you begin this lab:

- The number assigned to your classroom domain: *y*
- Your student number: *z*

**Estimated time to complete the lab: 1 hour 15 minutes**

# Exercise 1
# Creating Local User Accounts

In this exercise, you will create and modify a local user account on your student computer.

▶  **To create local user accounts**

1. Log on to Domain*y* (where *y* is the domain number) from your student computer as Student*z* (where *z* is your student number).

2. From the desktop, right-click My Computer, and then click Manage.

3. In the left pane of the Computer Management window, expand Computer Management (Local), expand System Tools, expand Local Users And Groups, and then select the Users folder.

4. From the Action menu, click New User.

5. In the New User dialog box, in the User Name box, type your first name, and in the Full Name box, type your full name.

6. In the Password and Confirm Password boxes, type the password you are using for your Student*z* account.

7. Clear the User Must Change Password At Next Logon check box, and then click Create.

    Another New User dialog box appears, indicating that the user has been created.

8. In the New User dialog box, click Close.

9. In the right pane of the Computer Management window, double-click the user account you just created.

10. In the user object's Properties dialog box, click the Member Of tab.

11. In the Member Of tab, click Add.

12. In the Select Groups dialog box, in the Name list, double-click Power Users, and then click OK.

    Which groups is the new user account a member of?

    _____

13. Click OK to close the user object's Properties dialog box.

14. Close the Computer Management window.

You have successfully created a new local user account on your computer and made that account a member of the Power Users group on your computer.

# Exercise 2
# Creating and Modifying Domain User Accounts

In this exercise, you will use Active Directory Users And Computers to create and modify a user account template and then use the template to create a domain user account.

▶ **To create and modify domain user accounts**

1. From the desktop, click Start, point to Programs, point to Administrative Tools, and then click MyCustomMMC.

2. In the left pane of the MyCustomMMC window, expand Active Directory Users And Computers, and then expand Domainy.com (where *y* is the domain number).

3. In the left pane, right-click OU*z* (where *z* is your student number), point to New, and then click User.

4. In the New Object – User dialog box, in the First Name box, type **Sales** and then in the Last Name box, type **Template**.

5. In the User Logon Name box, type **SalesTemplatez** (where z is your student number).

6. Click Next.

7. In the next New Object – User dialog box, type **C0mPlex** in both the Password and Confirm Password boxes, and then click Next.

8. In the next New Object – User dialog box, click Finish.

9. In the right pane of the MyCustomMMC window, double-click the user account you just created.

10. In the Sales Template Properties dialog box, click the Address tab.

11. In the Address tab, type your school or company's address information in the appropriate boxes. For the sake of demonstration later, enter information in the Street field as well as at least some of the other boxes.

12. Click the Member Of tab.

13. In the Member Of tab, click Add.

14. In the Select Groups dialog box, double-click the Users group, double-click the Guests group, and then click OK.

15. Click the Account tab.

16. In the Account tab, in the Account Options box, select the Account Is Disabled check box, and then click OK to close the Sales Template Properties dialog box.

17. In the right pane of the MyCustomMMC window, right-click the Sales Template user account, and then click Copy.

18. In the Copy Object – User dialog box, type your first and last names in the respective First Name and Last Name boxes.

19. In the User Logon Name box, type your first name and the first letter of your last name, and then click Next.

20. In the next Copy Object – User dialog box, type **OldPassw0rd** in the Password and Confirm Password boxes.

21. Clear the Account Is Disabled check box, and then click Next.

22. In the next Copy Object – User dialog box, click Finish.

23. In the right pane of the MyCustomMMC window, double-click the new domain user account you just created.

24. In the user object's Properties dialog box, click the Member Of tab.

    Which groups is the new account a member of?

    _____

    _____

25. In the user object's Properties dialog box, click the Address tab.

    Which part of the address information was copied to the new account?
    Which part of the address information was not copied to the new account?

    _____

    _____

    _____

26. In the user object's Properties dialog box, click OK.

27. Close MyCustomMMC.

You have successfully created and modified a user account to use as a template, and then created a new domain user account by copying the template account.

# Exercise 3
# Maintaining Domain User Accounts

In this exercise, you will disable a domain user account, enable a domain user account, and then reset the password on a domain user account.

▶  **To disable a user account**

1. From the desktop, click Start, point to Programs, point to Administrative Tools, and then click MyCustomMMC.

2. In the left pane of the MyCustomMMC window, expand Active Directory Users And Computers and Domain*y*.com (where *y* is the domain number), if they are not already expanded, and then click OU*z* (where *z* is your student number).

3. In the right pane of the MyCustomMMC window, right-click the user account with your name that you created in Exercise 2, and then click Disable Account.

   An Active Directory message box indicates that the account is now disabled.

4. In the Active Directory message box, click OK.

   How does Active Directory Users And Computers indicate that a user account has been disabled?

   _____

   _____

You have successfully disabled a user account. Users will not be able to log on using that user account until it is enabled again.

▶  **To enable a user account**

1. In the right pane of the MyCustomMMC window, right-click the user account you just disabled, and then click Enable Account.

2. In the Active Directory message box, click OK.

   An Active Directory message box indicates that the account is now enabled.

You have successfully enabled a user account. Users are now able to log on using that user account.

▶ **To reset the password for a user account**

1. In the right pane of the MyCustomMMC window, right click the user account you just enabled, and then click Reset Password.

2. In the Reset Password dialog box, type **NewPa$$word** in the New Password and Confirm Password boxes.

3. Select the User Must Change Password At Next Logon check box, and then click OK.

4. In the Active Directory message box, click OK.

5. Close MyCustomMMC.

You have successfully reset the password for a user account.

# Exercise 4
# Configuring Roaming User Profiles

In this exercise, you will configure roaming user profiles.

▶ **To create a shared folder to contain the roaming profiles**

1. From the desktop, click Start, point to Programs, point to Administrative Tools, and then click MyCustomMMC.

2. In the left pane of the MyCustomMMC window, expand Computer Management (Local), expand System Tools, expand Shared Folders, and then click Shares.

3. In the left pane, right-click Shares, and then click New File Share.

4. In the Create Shared Folder dialog box, type **C:\Profiles** in the Folder To Share box, then type **Profiles** in the Share Name box, and then click Next.

5. In the Create Shared Folder dialog box, click Yes to create the C:\Profiles folder.

6. In the next Create Shared Folder dialog box, select the All Users Have Full Control option, and then click Finish.

7. In the next Create Shared Folder dialog box (asking whether you want to create another folder), click No.

You have created and shared a folder to contain the roaming profiles.

▶ **To configure user accounts to use a roaming profile**

1. In the left pane of the MyCustomMMC window, expand Active Directory Users And Computers and Domainy.com (where *y* is the domain number), if they are not already expanded, and then click OU*z* (where *z* is your student number).

2. In the right pane, double-click the user account with your name that you created in Exercise 2.

3. In the user object's Properties dialog box, click the Profile tab.

4. In the Profile tab, in the Profile Path box, type **\\Serverz\Profiles \%USERNAME%** (where *z* is your student number), and then click OK.

5. In the right pane of the MyCustomMMC window, double-click the Sales Template user account.

6. In the Sales Template Properties dialog box, click the Profile tab.

7. In the Profile tab, in the Profile Path box, type **\\Serverz\Profiles \%USERNAME%** and then click OK.

8. Close the MyCustomMMC window.

You have modified the user profile path for your user account and for the Sales Template user account. Any users that you create by using the Sales Template account from now on will have the updated user profile path.

▶ **To configure NT file system (NTFS) permissions for the Profiles shared folder**

1. From the desktop, right-click My Computer, and then click Explore.
2. In the left pane of the My Computer window, expand Local Disk (C:), and then click the Profiles folder.
3. From the File menu, click Properties.
4. In the Profiles Properties dialog box, click the Security tab.
5. In the Security tab, click the Everyone group, and then in the Permissions box, click the Allow check box next to the Full Control permission.
6. Click OK.
7. Close Windows Explorer.
8. Log off your computer as Student*z*.

You have successfully configured permissions for the Profiles shared folder.

▶ **To view the contents of a roaming profile**

1. Log on to Domain*y* (where *y* is the domain number) from your student computer as the user account you created in Exercise 2 (named with your first name and the first letter of your last name), using a password of **NewPa$$word**.
2. In the Logon Message message box, click OK.
3. In the Change Password dialog box, type a new complex password in the New Password and Confirm New Password boxes, and then click OK.
4. In the Change Password message box, click OK.
5. Log off, and then log on again to Domain*y* as the user account you created in Exercise 2, using the complex password you assigned in step 3 of this procedure.

**Note** When you logged off the computer, your roaming user profile folder was created and saved in the Profiles shared folder.

6. From the desktop, right-click My Computer, and then click Explore.
7. In the left pane of the My Computer window, expand Local Disk (C:), expand the Profiles folder, and then click the folder corresponding to your username (the first name and last initial).
8. Click the Tools menu, and then click Folder Options.
9. In the Folder Options dialog box, click the View tab.

10. In the View tab, in the Advanced settings box, click the Show Hidden Files And Folders option, then clear the Hide File Extensions For Known File Types check box, and then click OK.

What does your roaming user profile folder contain?

_____

_____

_____

_____

_____

11. Close Windows Explorer.

You have successfully shared a user profile folder, assigned a roaming user profile to a user account, and then viewed the contents of the roaming user profile.

# Lab 8: Managing Group Accounts

## Objectives

After completing this lab, you will be able to

- Create and modify group accounts in the domain
- Create and modify local group accounts
- Use the Run As program to run programs as Administrator

---

**Note** Completing this lab will help reinforce your learning from Chapter 8 of the textbook.

---

## Before You Begin

This lab is dependent on Lab 1. Lab 1 must be completed before you begin this lab.

You will need to get the following information from your instructor before you begin this lab:

- The number assigned to your classroom domain: $y$
- Your student number: $z$

**Estimated time to complete the lab: 60 minutes**

# Exercise 1
# Creating and Modifying Group Accounts in the Domain

In this exercise, you will use Active Directory Users And Computers to create several group accounts in the domain, and then you will add members to these groups.

▶  **To create a domain local group**

1. Log on to Domain*y* (where *y* is the domain number) from your student computer as Student*z* (where *z* is your student number).

2. From the desktop, click Start, point to Programs, point to Administrative Tools, and then click MyCustomMMC.

3. In the left pane of the MyCustomMMC window, expand Active Directory Users And Computers and Domain*y*.com (if they are not already expanded), and then click OU*z*.

4. From the Action menu, point to New, and then click Group.

5. In the New Object – Group dialog box, in the Group Name box, type **DomLocal*z***.

6. In the Group Scope section, select the Domain Local option; then in the Group Type section, select the Security option, and then click OK.

   The new group appears in the right pane of the MyCustomMMC window.

   What information is listed in the Type column of the window for the group you just created?

   _____

▶  **To create a global group**

1. In the left pane of the MyCustomMMC window, right-click OU*z* (where *z* is your student number), point to New, and then click Group.

2. In the New Object – Group dialog box, in the Group Name box, type **Global*z***.

3. In the Group Scope section, select the Global option; then in the Group Type section, select the Security option, and then click OK.

   The new group appears in the right pane of the MyCustomMMC window.

   What information is listed in the Type column of the window for the group you just created?

   _____

▶ **To create a universal group**

1. In the left pane of the MyCustomMMC window, right-click OU*z* (where *z* is your student number), point to New, and then click Group.

2. In the New Object – Group dialog box, in the Group Name box, type **Universal*z***.

3. In the Group Scope section, select the Universal option; then in the Group Type section, select the Security option, and then click OK.

   The new group appears in the right pane of the MyCustomMMC window.

   What information is listed in the Type column of the window for the group you just created?

   _____

▶ **To add members to groups**

1. In the right pane of the MyCustomMMC window, double-click Universal*z* (where *z* is your student number).

2. In the Universal*z* Properties dialog box, click the Members tab.

3. In the Members tab, click Add.

4. In the Select Users, Contacts, Computers, Or Groups dialog box, in the Name list, double-click the user account with your name, and then click OK.

5. In the Universal*z* Properties dialog box, click OK.

6. In the right pane of the MyCustomMMC window, double-click Global*z*.

7. In the Global*z* Properties dialog box, click the Members tab.

8. In the Members tab, click Add.

9. In the Select Users, Contacts, Computers, Or Groups dialog box, in the Name list, double-click User*z*, and then click OK.

10. In the Global*z* Properties dialog box, click OK.

11. In the right pane of the MyCustomMMC window, double-click DomLocal*z*.

12. In the DomLocal*z* Properties dialog box, click the Members tab.

13. In the Members tab, click Add.

14. In the Select Users, Contacts, Computers, Or Groups dialog box, in the Name list, double-click Global*z*, and then click OK.

15. In the DomLocal*z* Properties dialog box, click OK.

16. Close the MyCustomMMC window.

You have successfully created a domain local group, a global group, and a universal group, and added members to each of these groups.

# Exercise 2
# Creating and Modifying Local Group Accounts

In this exercise, you will create a local group account on your student computer and add members to it.

▶   **To create and modify local group accounts**

1.  From the desktop, right-click My Computer, and then click Manage.

2.  In the Computer Management window, expand Local Users And Groups, and then click the Groups folder.

3.  Click the Action menu, and then click New Group.

4.  In the New Group dialog box, in the Group Name box, type **ComputerLocal** and then click Add.

5.  In the Select Users Or Groups dialog box, in the Look In list, select Domain*y*.com (where *y* is the domain number).

6.  In the Select Users Or Groups dialog box, in the Name list, double-click the Global*z* and Universal*z* groups (where *z* is your student number), and then click OK.

7.  In the New Group dialog box, click Create, and then click Close.

8.  Close the Computer Management window.

You have successfully created a new local group on your computer and have added the global and universal groups you created in Exercise 1 to this new local group.

# Exercise 3
# Using the Run As Program

In this exercise, you will log on as a regular user and then use the Run As program to start a program as Administrator.

▶   **To use the Run As program**

1. Log off your computer, and then log on to Domain*y* (where *y* is the domain number) from your student computer as User*z* (where *z* is your student number).

2. From the desktop, click Start, point to Programs, point to Administrative Tools, and then click Computer Management.

3. In the Computer Management window, expand Local Users And Groups, and then click the Groups folder.

4. From the Action menu, click New Group.

5. In the New Group dialog box, in the Group Name box, type **TestGroup** and then click Create.

   What error is listed in the Local Users And Groups message box?

   _____

   _____

   Why was this error displaycd?

   _____

   _____

6. In the Local Users And Groups message box, click OK.

7. In the New Group dialog box, click Close.

8. Close the Computer Management window.

9. From the desktop, press and hold the SHIFT key; then click Start, point to Programs, point to Administrative Tools, right-click Computer Management, and then click Run As.

10. In the Run As Other User dialog box, select Run The Program As The Following User.

11. In the User Name box, type **Student*z***.

12. In the Password box, type your password.

13. In the Domain box, type **Domain*y*** and then click OK.

14. In the Computer Management window, expand Local Users And Groups, and then click the Groups folder.

15. From the Action menu, click New Group.

16. In the New Group dialog box, in the Group Name box, type **TestGroup** and then click Create, and then click Close.

    Were you able to successfully create the new group? Why or why not?

    _____

    _____

    _____

17. Close the Computer Management window.

You have attempted to create a group by using Computer Management while logged on as a user who is not a member of the Administrators or Domain Admins group, but you were unsuccessful in creating a group. Then you used the Run As program to run the Computer Management program as a user account that is a member of the Domain Admins group, and you were able to successfully create a group.

# Lab 9: Managing Group Policy

## Objectives

After completing this lab, you will be able to

- Configure and apply local policy
- Configure, apply, and filter group policy for an organizational unit (OU)

---

**Note** Completing this lab will help reinforce your learning from Chapter 9 of the textbook.

---

## Before You Begin

This lab is dependent on Lab 1 and Lab 6. Lab 1 and Lab 6 must be completed before you begin this lab.

You will need to get the following information from your instructor before you begin this lab:

- The number assigned to your classroom domain: $y$
- Your student number: $z$

**Estimated time to complete the lab: 60 minutes**

# Exercise 1
# Configuring and Applying Local Policy

In this exercise, you will use the Local Computer Policy preconfigured console to configure and apply local policy settings on your student computer.

▶ **To configure and apply local policy**

1. Log on to Domain*y* (where *y* is the domain number) from your student computer as Student*z* (where *z* is your student number).

2. From the desktop, click Start.

   Which options are listed in the Start menu?

   _____

   _____

   _____

   _____

3. From the Start menu, click Run.

4. In the Run dialog box, in the Open box, type **Gpedit.msc** to open the Group Policy window, and then click OK.

5. In the left pane of the Group Policy window, in the User Configuration section, expand Administrative Templates, and then click Start Menu & Taskbar.

6. In the right pane of the Group Policy window, double-click Remove Documents Menu From Start Menu.

7. In the Remove Documents Menu From Start Menu Properties dialog box, select Enabled, and then click OK.

8. In the right pane of the Group Policy window, double-click Remove Search Menu From Start Menu.

9. In the Remove Search Menu From Start Menu Properties dialog box, select Enabled, and then click OK.

10. In the right pane of the Group Policy window, double-click Add Logoff To The Start Menu.

11. In the Add Logoff To The Start Menu Properties dialog box, select Enabled, and then click OK.

    Notice that the status of the three items you modified has changed in the Settings column from Not Configured to Enabled.

12. Close the Group Policy window.

13. From the Desktop, click Start.

    Which options have been removed from the Start menu?

    _____

    _____

    Which option has been added to the Start menu?

    _____

    _____

14. Press Esc to close the Start menu.

You have successfully configured and applied local policy and have viewed the results on your computer.

# Exercise 2
# Configuring, Applying, and Filtering Group Policy for an OU

In this exercise, you will use Active Directory Users And Computers to configure a group policy object (GPO) for an OU in the Active Directory service, configure filtering for the GPO, and then apply that GPO to your computer.

▶ **To create a security group for filtering group policy**

1. From the desktop, click Start, point to Programs, point to Administrative Tools, and then click MyCustomMMC.

2. In the left pane of the MyCustomMMC window, expand Active Directory Users And Computers and Domain$y$.com (where $y$ is the domain number), if they are not already expanded, and then select OU$z$ (where $z$ is your student number).

3. Click the Action menu, point to New, and then click Group.

4. In the New Object – Group dialog box, type **No OU$z$ Policy** in the Group Name box, select the Global option in the Group Scope box, select the Security option in the Group Type box, and then click OK.

5. In the right pane of the MyCustomMMC window, double-click the No OU$z$ Policy group.

6. In the No OU$z$ Policy Properties dialog box, click the Members tab.

7. In the Members tab, click Add.

8. In the Select Users, Contacts, Computers, Or Groups dialog box, double-click User$z$, and then click OK.

9. In the No OU$z$ Policy Properties dialog box, click OK.

You have successfully created a security group and added a member to the group. This security group will be used to filter the application of the GPO that you will create in the next procedure.

▶ **To create a GPO and configure filtering**

1. In the left pane of the MyCustomMMC window, right-click OU$z$ (where $z$ is your student number), and then click Properties.

2. In the OU$z$ Properties dialog box, click the Group Policy tab.

3. In the Group Policy tab, click New, and name the new group policy object **OU$z$ Policy.**

4. In the Group Policy tab, click Properties.

5. In the OU$z$ Policy Properties dialog box, click the Security tab.

6. In the Security tab, click Add.

7. In the Select Users, Computers, Or Groups dialog box, double-click the No OU*z* Policy group, and then click OK.

8. In the OU*z* Policy Properties dialog box, in the Security tab, select the No OU*z* Policy group in the Name list.

9. In the Security tab, in the Permissions box, select the Deny check boxes next to Read and Apply Group Policy, and then click OK.

10. In the Security message box, click Yes.

You have successfully created a GPO and configured filtering by denying the No OU*z* Policy group the Read and Apply Group Policy permissions to the GPO.

▶  **To configure group policy settings**

1. In the OU*z* Properties dialog box (where *z* is your student number), in the Group Policy tab, select OU*z* Policy, and then click Edit.

2. In the left pane of the Group Policy window, in the Computer Configuration section, expand Windows Settings, expand Security Settings, expand Local Policies, and then select Security Options.

3. In the right pane, double-click Message Text For Users Attempting To Log On.

4. In the Security Policy Setting dialog box, select the check box next to Define This Policy Setting.

5. In the Security Policy Setting dialog box, in the Define This Policy Setting box, type **Do not log on to this computer unless you are an employee of the XYZ Company!** and then click OK.

6. In the right pane, double-click Message Title For Users Attempting To Log On.

7. In the Security Policy Setting dialog box, select the check box next to Define This Policy Setting.

8. In the Security Policy Setting dialog box, in the Define This Policy Setting box, type **Legal Notice** and then click OK.

   Notice that the message text and title you typed are now displayed in the Settings column next to the respective items.

9. In the left pane of the Group Policy window, in the User Configuration section, expand Administrative Templates, and then select Start Menu & Taskbar.

10. In the right pane of the Group Policy window, double-click Remove Documents Menu From Start Menu.

11. In the Remove Documents Menu From Start Menu Properties dialog box, select the Disabled option, and then click OK.

12. In the right pane of the Group Policy window, double-click Remove Search Menu From Start Menu.

13. In the Remove Search Menu From Start Menu Properties dialog box, select the Disabled option, and then click OK

    Notice that the status of the two items you modified has changed in the Settings column from Not Configured to Disabled.

14. Close the Group Policy window.

15. In the OUz Properties dialog box, click Close.

16. Close the MyCustomMMC window.

You have configured several settings in the GPO. In the next section, you will see how these polices are applied.

► **To apply group policy**

1. From the desktop, click Start, and then click Run.

2. In the Run dialog box, in the Open box, type **secedit /refreshpolicy machine_policy** and then click OK.

    This command-line utility refreshes the security settings on the computer.

3. Click Start, and then click Log Off Studentz (where z is your student number).

4. In the Log Off Windows dialog box, click Yes.

5. When the Welcome To Windows dialog box appears, press CTRL+ALT+DELETE.

    What is the title of the message box that appears?

    _____

    What does the text in the message box say?

    _____

    _____

6. In the Legal Notice message box, click OK.

7. Log on to Domainy (where y is the domain number) from your student computer as Studentz.

8. Click Start.

    Which options have been added to the Start menu?

    _____

    _____

Why were these options added to the Start menu?

_____

_____

_____

_____

_____

9. Log off your computer.

10. Log on to Domainy from your student computer as Userz.

11. From the desktop, click Start.

How is the Start menu different from the Start menu that Studentz had in step 8?

_____

_____

Why did this happen?

_____

_____

12. Log off your computer.

You have successfully applied group policy to your computer and viewed the results of the group policy. In addition, the group policy was filtered, and you logged on as a user the policy did not apply to and viewed the results of filtering group policy.

# Lab 10: Using Group Policy to Publish Resources, Redirect Folders, and Deploy Applications

## Objectives

After completing this lab, you will be able to

- Publish a shared folder in the Active Directory service
- Search Active Directory for shared folders and shared printers
- Redirect users' \My Documents folders to a shared folder on the network
- Deploy, upgrade, and remove applications

---

**Note** Completing this lab will help reinforce your learning from Chapter 10 of the textbook.

---

## Before You Begin

This lab is dependent on Lab 1, Lab 5, and Lab 6. Lab 1, Lab 5, and Lab 6 must be completed before you begin this lab.

You will need to get the following information from your instructor before you begin this lab:

- The number assigned to your instructor's computer: $x$
- The number assigned to your classroom domain: $y$
- Your student number: $z$

**Estimated time to complete the lab: 1 hour 10 minutes**

# Exercise 1
# Publishing a Shared Folder in Active Directory

In this exercise, you will use Active Directory Users And Computers to publish a distributed file system (Dfs) root as a shared folder in Active Directory.

▶ **To publish a shared folder in Active Directory**

1. Log on to Domain*y* (where *y* is the domain number) from your student computer as Student*z* (where *z* is your student number).

2. From the desktop, click Start, point to Programs, point to Administrative Tools, and then click MyCustomMMC.

3. In the left pane of the MyCustomMMC window, expand Active Directory Users And Computers and Domain*y*.com, if they are not already expanded, and then select OU*z*.

4. On the Action menu, point to New, and then click Shared Folder.

5. In the New Object – Shared Folder dialog box, in the Name box, type **MyDfs*z***.

6. In the Network path box, type **\\Server*z*\MyDfs** and then click OK.

7. Close the MyCustomMMC window.

You have successfully published a shared folder in Active Directory.

# Exercise 2
# Searching Active Directory for Shared Folders and Shared Printers

In this exercise, you will use the Search function in the Start menu to search Active Directory for shared folders and shared printers.

▶ **To search Active Directory for shared folders and shared printers**

1. From the desktop, right-click My Computer, and then click Explore.

2. In the left pane of the My Computer window, expand My Network Places and Entire Network (if they are not already expanded), and then select Directory.

3. In the right pane, right-click Domain*y* (where *y* is the domain number), and then click Find.

4. In the Find Users, Contacts, And Groups dialog box, in the Find box, select Shared Folders, and then click Find Now.

   Which shared folders are listed in Active Directory?

   _____

   _____

   _____

5. In the Find Users, Contacts, And Groups dialog box, in the Find box, select Printers.

6. In the Find In The Directory message box, click OK.

7. In the Find Printers dialog box, click Find Now.

   Which printers are listed in Active Directory?

   _____

   _____

   _____

8. Close the Find Printers dialog box.

9. Close Windows Explorer.

You have successfully searched Active Directory for shared folders and shared printers.

# Exercise 3
# Redirecting Users' \My Documents Folders to a Shared Folder on the Network

In this exercise, you will use Active Directory Users And Computers to configure group policy settings to redirect users' \My Documents folders to a shared folder on the network.

▶ **To redirect users' \My Documents folders to a shared folder on the network**

1. From the desktop, click Start, point to Programs, point to Administrative Tools, and then click MyCustomMMC.

2. In the left pane of the MyCustomMMC window, expand Active Directory Users And Computers and Domain$y$.com (where $y$ is the domain number), if they are not already expanded, then right-click OU$z$ (where $z$ is your student number), and then click Properties.

3. In the OU$z$ Properties dialog box, click the Group Policy tab.

4. In the Group Policy tab, in the Group Policy Object Links list, click OU$z$ Policy, and then click Edit.

5. In the left pane of the Group Policy window, in the User Configuration section, expand Windows Settings and Folder Redirection (if not already expanded), then right-click My Documents, and then click Properties.

6. In the My Documents Properties dialog box, in the Setting list, select Basic – Redirect Everyone's Folder To The Same Location.

7. In the Target Folder Location box, type **\\Server$z$\SharedData \%USERNAME%\My Documents** and then click OK.

8. Close the Group Policy window.

9. In the OU$z$ Properties dialog box, click OK.

10. Close the MyCustomMMC window.

11. Log off, and then log on to Domain$y$ from your student computer as Student$z$.

12. From the desktop, right-click My Documents, and then click Properties.

    What is the target folder location for the \My Documents folder on the desktop?

    _____

    _____

13. In the My Documents Properties dialog box, click OK.

You have successfully redirected the \My Documents folder for all of the users in OU$z$.

# Exercise 4
# Deploying, Upgrading, and Removing Applications

In this exercise, you will use group policy to deploy Adminpak.msi and then to deploy, upgrade, and remove the Cosmo application on your student computer.

▶ **To deploy Adminpak.msi to your student computer**

1. From the desktop, click Start, point to Programs, and then point to Administrative Tools.

   Which programs are listed in the Administrative Tools folder?

   _____

   _____

   _____

   _____

   _____

   _____

2. In the left pane of the MyCustomMMC window, expand Active Directory Users And Computers and Domain*y*.com (where *y* is the domain number), if they are not already expanded, then right-click OU*z* (where *z* is your student number), and then click Properties.

3. In the OU*z* Properties dialog box, click the Group Policy tab.

4. In the Group Policy tab, in the Group Policy Object Links list, click OU*z* Policy, and then click Edit.

5. In the left pane of the Group Policy window, in the Computer Configuration section, click Software Settings.

6. In the right pane, right-click Software Installation, point to New, and then click Package.

7. In the Open dialog box, in the File Name box, type **\\Instructor.*x*\W2000Srv\I386\Adminpak.msi** (where *x* is the number assigned to your instructor's computer) and then click Open.

8. In the Deploy Software dialog box, select Assigned, and then click OK.

9. Close the Group Policy window.

10. In the OU*z* Properties dialog box, click OK.

11. Close the MyCustomMMC window.

12. Shut down and restart your computer.

A status message appears that says Installing Managed Software Windows 2000 Administration Tools.

13. Log on to Domain*y* from your student computer as Student*z*.

14. Click Start, point to Programs, and then point to Administrative Tools.

Are any new programs listed?

_____

You have successfully deployed the Microsoft Windows 2000 Administrative Tools (the Adminpak) to your computer by using group policy.

▶ **To deploy the Cosmo application to all of the users in an organizational unit (OU)**

1. From the desktop, click Start, point to Programs, point to Administrative Tools, and then click MyCustomMMC.

2. In the left pane of the MyCustomMMC window, expand Active Directory Users And Computers and Domain*y*.com (where *y* is the domain number), if they are not already expanded, then right-click OU*z* (where *z* is your student number), and then click Properties.

3. In the OU*z* Properties dialog box, click the Group Policy tab.

4. In the Group Policy tab, in the Group Policy Object Links list, click OU*z* Policy, and then click Edit.

5. In the left pane of the Group Policy window, in the User Configuration section, select Software Settings.

6. In the right pane, right-click Software Installation, point to New, and then click Package.

7. In the Open dialog box, in the File Name box, type **\\Instructor*x*\LabFiles \COSMO1\Cosmo1.msi** (where *x* is the number assigned to your instructor's computer), and then click Open.

8. In the Deploy Software dialog box, select Published, and then click OK.

9. Close the Group Policy window.

10. In the OU*z* Properties dialog box, click OK.

11. Close the MyCustomMMC window.

12. Log off, and then log on to Domain*y* from your student computer as Student*z*.

13. Click Start, point to Settings, and then click Control Panel.

14. In the Control Panel window, double-click Add/Remove Programs.

15. In the Add/Remove Programs dialog box, click Add New Programs.

16. In the Add Programs From Your Network box, select Cosmo 1, and then click Add.

17. In the Cosmo 1 message box, click OK.

18. In the Add/Remove Programs dialog box, click Close.

19. Close Control Panel.

20. Click Start, point to Programs, point to Cosmo, and then click Cosmo v 1.0.

    The Cosmo application starts.

21. Close the Cosmo – 00 window.

You have successfully used group policy to publish the Cosmo 1 application to all of the users in an OU.

▶   **To deploy an upgrade to the Cosmo application**

1. From the desktop, click Start, point to Programs, point to Administrative Tools, and then click MyCustomMMC.

2. In the left pane of the MyCustomMMC window, expand Active Directory Users And Computers and Domain*y*.com (where *y* is the domain number), if they are not already expanded, then right-click OU*z* (where *z* is your student number), and then click Properties.

3. In the OU*z* Properties dialog box, click the Group Policy tab.

4. In the Group Policy tab, in the Group Policy Object Links list, select OU*z* Policy, and then click Edit.

5. In the left pane of the Group Policy window, in the User Configuration section, select Software Settings.

6. In the right pane, right-click Software Installation, point to New, and then click Package.

7. In the Open dialog box, in the File Name box, type **\\Instructor*x*\LabFiles \COSMO2\Cosmo2.msi** (where *x* is the number assigned to your instructor's computer), and then click Open.

8. In the Deploy Software dialog box, select Advanced Published Or Assigned, and then click OK.

9. In the Cosmo 2 Properties dialog box, click the Upgrades tab.

10. In the Upgrades tab, click Add.

11. In the Add Upgrade Package dialog box, in the Package To Upgrade box, select Cosmo 1, select Uninstall The Existing Package, Then Install The Upgrade Package, and then click OK.

12. In the Cosmo 2 Properties dialog box, in the Upgrades tab, select the check box next to Required Upgrade For Existing Packages, and then click OK.

13. Close the Group Policy window.

14. In the OU*z* Properties dialog box, click OK.

15. Close the MyCustomMMC window.

16. Log off, and then log on to Domain*y* from your student computer as Student*z*.

17. Click Start, point to Programs, point to Cosmo, and then click Cosmo v 2.0.

    Cosmo v 2.0 is installed and the application starts.

18. Close the Cosmo – 15 window.

You have successfully used group policy to upgrade the Cosmo 1 application to Cosmo 2.

▶   **To remove the Cosmo application**

1. From the desktop, click Start, point to Programs, point to Administrative Tools, and then click MyCustomMMC.

2. In the left pane of the MyCustomMMC window, expand Active Directory Users And Computers and Domain*y*.com (where *y* is the domain number), if they are not already expanded, then right-click OU*z* (where *z* is your student number), and then click Properties.

3. In the OU*z* Properties dialog box, click the Group Policy tab.

4. In the Group Policy tab, in the Group Policy Object Links list, select OU*z* Policy, and then click Edit.

5. In the left pane of the Group Policy window, in the User Configuration section, expand Software Settings (if it is not already expanded), and then select Software Installation.

6. In the right pane, right-click the Cosmo 1 application, point to All Tasks, and then click Remove.

7. In the Remove Software dialog box, select Immediately Uninstall The Software From Users And Computers, and then click OK.

8. In the right pane, right-click the Cosmo 2 application, point to All Tasks, and then click Remove.

9. In the Remove Software dialog box, select Immediately Uninstall The Software From Users And Computers, and then click OK.

10. Close the Group Policy window.

11. In the OU*z* Properties dialog box, click OK.

12. Close the MyCustomMMC window.

13. Log off, and then log on to Domain*y* from your student computer as Student*z*.

14. Click Start, and then point to Programs.

    Is the Cosmo program group still available?

You have successfully removed the Cosmo application, which you previously deployed and upgraded, by using group policy.

# Lab 11: Configuring Replication

## Objectives

After completing this lab, you will be able to

- Create a site
- Create a subnet object
- Create and configure a site link
- Create a site link bridge
- Check the replication topology

**Note** Completing this lab will help reinforce your learning from Chapter 11 of the textbook.

## Before You Begin

This lab is dependent on Lab 1 and Lab 6. Lab 1 and Lab 6 must be completed before you begin this lab.

You will need to get the following information from your instructor before you begin this lab:

- The number assigned to your instructor's computer: $x$
- The number assigned to your classroom domain: $y$
- Your student number: $z$

**Estimated time to complete the lab: 40 minutes**

# Exercise 1
# Using Active Directory Sites And Services to Configure Replication

In this exercise, you will use Active Directory Sites And Services to create Active Directory objects that are used in the replication process. You will also use Active Directory Sites And Services to check the replication topology.

▶ **To create a site**

1. Log on to Domain*y* (where *y* is the domain number) from your student computer as Student*z* (where *z* is your student number).

2. From the desktop, click Start, point to Programs, point to Administrative Tools, right-click Active Directory Sites And Services, and then click Sort By Name.

   This sorts all of the shortcuts in the Administrative Tools folder so that MyCustomMMC is listed in alphabetical order.

3. From the desktop, click Start, point to Programs, point to Administrative Tools, right-click MyCustomMMC, and then click Author.

   Opening MyCustomMMC in Author mode allows you to add or remove snap-ins.

4. In the MyCustomMMC window, on the Console menu, click Add/Remove Snap-In.

5. In the Add/Remove Snap-In dialog box, click Add.

6. In the Add Standalone Snap-In dialog box, click Active Directory Sites And Services, click Add, and then click Close.

7. In the Add/Remove Snap-In dialog box, click OK.

8. In the MyCustomMMC window, on the Console menu, click Save.

9. In the left pane of the MyCustomMMC window, expand Active Directory Sites And Services, and then expand Sites.

10. In the left pane of the MyCustomMMC window, right-click Sites, and then click New Site.

11. In the New Object – Site dialog box, in the Name box, type **Site***z* and then in the Link Name list, select DEFAULTIPSITELINK, and then click OK.

    An Active Directory message box appears, providing instructions for the rest of the site configuration process.

12. In the Active Directory message box, click OK.

You have successfully created a new site in Active Directory. In the next procedure, you will create a new subnet object and associate that subnet object with the site you just created.

▶ **To create a subnet object**

1. In the left pane of the MyCustomMMC window, under Active Directory Sites And Services, expand Sites, and then click Subnets.

2. On the Action menu, click New Subnet.

3. In the New Object – Subnet dialog box, in the Address box, type **10.100.$z$.0** (where $z$ is your student number); then in the Mask box, type **255.255.255.0**; then in the Site Name list, select Site$z$, and then click OK.

You have successfully created a new subnet object and associated it with the site you created in the first section of this exercise. Next, you will create a site link between the site you just created and the Default-First-Site-Name site.

▶ **To create and configure a site link**

1. In the left pane of the MyCustomMMC window, under Active Directory Sites And Services, expand Inter-Site Transports, and then click IP.

2. On the Action menu, click New Site Link.

3. In the New Object – Site Link dialog box, in the Name box, type **SiteLink$z$** (where $z$ is your student number).

4. In the Sites Not In This Site Link box, click Default-First-Site-Name, and then click Add.

   Default-First-Site-Name moves to the Sites In This Site Link box.

5. In the Sites Not In This Site Link box, click Site$z$, click Add, and then click OK.

   Site$z$ moves to the Sites In This Site Link box.

6. In the right pane of the MyCustomMMC window, double-click SiteLink$z$.

7. In the SiteLink$z$ Properties dialog box, in the Cost box, configure a cost of 125.

8. In the Replicate Every box, configure a replication frequency of 240 minutes (4 hours), and then click Change Schedule.

9. In the Schedule For SiteLink$z$ dialog box, select Monday through Friday from 8 A.M. to 10 A.M.

10. Select Replication Not Available, and then click OK.

11. In the SiteLink$z$ Properties dialog box, click OK.

You have successfully created a site link, associated the site link with two sites, configured a cost for the link, configured the replication frequency for the link, and modified the replication schedule for the link so that replication cannot occur over the link between 8 A.M. and 10 A.M. Monday through Friday.

▶ **To create a site link bridge**

1. In the left pane of the MyCustomMMC window, under Active Directory Sites And Services, right-click IP, and then click New Site Link Bridge.

2. In the New Object – Site Link Bridge dialog box, in the Name box, type **SiteLinkBridge**z (where z is your student number).

3. In the Site Links Not In This Site Link Bridge list, select SiteLinkz, and then click Add.

   SiteLinkz moves to the Sites In This Site Link Bridge box.

4. Close the MyCustomMMC window.

   DEFAULTIPSITELINK moves to the Sites In This Site Link Bridge box.

You have successfully created a site link bridge that bridges the site link you created earlier with DEFAULTIPSITELINK.

▶ **To force the Knowledge Consistency Checker to check the replication topology**

1. In the left pane of the MyCustomMMC window, under Active Directory Sites And Services, expand Default-First-Site-Name, expand Servers, and then click Instructorx (where x is the number of your instructor's computer).

2. In the right pane, right-click NTDS Settings, point to All Tasks, and then click Check Replication Topology.

   What message appears in the Check Replication Topology message box?

   _____

   _____

3. In the Check Replication Topology message box, click OK.

4. Close MyCustomMMC.

5. In the Microsoft Management Console message box, click Yes.

You have successfully forced the Knowledge Consistency Checker (KCC) to check the replication topology.

# Lab 12: Administering Active Directory

## Objectives

After completing this lab, you will be able to

- Configure permissions for Active Directory objects
- Search the Active Directory service
- Move Active Directory objects
- Use the Delegation Of Control Wizard

---

**Note** Completing this lab will help reinforce your learning from Chapter 12 of the textbook.

---

## Before You Begin

This lab is dependent on Lab 1, Lab 5, Lab 6, and Lab 10. Lab 1, Lab 5, Lab 6, and Lab 10 must be completed before you begin this lab.

You will need to get the following information from your instructor before you begin this lab:

- The number assigned to your classroom domain: $y$
- Your student number: $z$

**Estimated time to complete the lab: 40 minutes**

# Exercise 1
# Configuring Permissions for Active Directory Objects

In this exercise, you will use Active Directory Users And Computers to configure permissions for an organizational unit (OU) in Active Directory.

▶ **To configure permissions for an Active Directory object**

1. Log on to Domain*y* (where *y* is the domain number) from your student computer as Student*z* (where *z* is your student number).

2. From the desktop, click Start, point to Programs, point to Administrative Tools, and then click MyCustomMMC.

3. In the left pane of the MyCustomMMC window, select Active Directory Users And Computers, and then, on the View menu, ensure that the Advanced Features option is selected.

4. In the left pane of the MyCustomMMC window, expand Active Directory Users And Computers and Domain*y*, and then select OU*z*.

5. Click the Action menu, and then click Properties.

6. In the OU*z* Properties dialog box, click the Security tab.

7. In the Security tab, click Add.

8. In the Select Users, Computers, Or Groups dialog box, in the Name list, double-click the user account with your first and last name, and then click OK.

9. In the OU*z* Properties dialog box, in the Permissions box, click the Allow Full Control check box, and then click Advanced.

10. In the Access Control Settings For OU*z* dialog box, select the user account with your name, and then click View/Edit.

    The Permission Entry For OU*z* window appears.

    Do the permissions that you just assigned to your user account apply to the OU only or to the OU and all of its child objects?

    _____

11. In the Permission Entry For OU*z* dialog box, in the Apply Onto list, select This Object And All Child Objects, and then click OK.

12. In the Access Control Settings For OU*z* dialog box, click OK.

13. In the OU*z* Properties dialog box, click OK.

14. Close the MyCustomMMC window.

You have successfully assigned the user account with your name the Full Control permissions to your student OU and all of its child objects.

# Exercise 2
# Searching Active Directory

In this exercise, you will use Active Directory Users And Computers to perform a basic and an advanced search of Active Directory.

▶ **To search Active Directory**

1. From the desktop, click Start, point to Programs, point to Administrative Tools, and then click MyCustomMMC.

2. In the left pane of the MyCustomMMC window, expand Active Directory Users And Computers (if it is not already expanded), and then select Domain*y* (where y is the domain number).

3. On the Action menu, click Find.

4. In the Find Users, Contacts And Groups dialog box, in the Name box, type your first name, and then click Find Now.

   What names are listed in the Name list at the bottom of the Find Users, Contacts, And Groups dialog box?

   _____

5. Double-click the user account in the Name list at the bottom of the Find Users, Contacts, And Groups dialog box.

   What dialog box appears?

   _____

6. In the dialog box that appears, click OK.

7. In the Find Users, Contacts And Groups dialog box, click Clear All.

8. In the Find In The Directory message box, click OK.

9. In the Find Users, Contacts And Groups dialog box, click the Advanced tab.

10. In the Find Users, Contacts And Groups dialog box, click Field, point to User, and then click Last Name.

11. In the Condition list, select Is (Exactly).

12. In the Value box, type your last name, click Add, and then click Find Now.

    What names are listed in the Name list at the bottom of the Find Users, Contacts, And Groups dialog box?

    _____

13. Close the Find Users, Contacts, And Groups dialog box.

14. Close the MyCustomMMC window.

You have successfully performed a basic search and an advanced search of Active Directory.

# Exercise 3
# Moving Active Directory Objects

In this exercise, you will use Active Directory Users And Computers to move an object in Active Directory.

▶ **To move an Active Directory object**

1. From the desktop, click Start, point to Programs, point to Administrative Tools, and then click MyCustomMMC.

2. In the left pane of the MyCustomMMC window, select Active Directory Users And Computers, and then, on the View menu, ensure that the Users, Groups, And Computers As Containers option is selected.

3. In the left pane of the MyCustomMMC window, expand Active Directory Users And Computers and Domain*y* (where *y* is the domain number), if they are not already expanded, and then click OU*z* (where *z* is your student number).

4. In the left pane of the MyCustomMMC window, expand OU*z*, and then select Server*z*.

5. In the right pane of the MyCustomMMC window, right-click the printer object that is displayed there, and then click Move.

6. In the Move dialog box, click OU*z*, and then click OK.

7. In the left pane of the MyCustomMMC window, click OU*z*.

   Is the printer object you just moved listed in the right pane?

   _____

8. Close the MyCustomMMC window.

You have successfully moved the printer object that you created and shared in Lab 5 into your student OU.

# Exercise 4
# Using the Delegation Of Control Wizard

In this exercise, you will use the Delegation Of Control Wizard in Active Directory Users And Computers to assign a user the appropriate permissions to reset passwords for all users in an OU.

▶ **To use the Delegation of Control Wizard**

1. From the desktop, click Start, point to Programs, point to Administrative Tools, and then click MyCustomMMC.

2. In the left pane of the MyCustomMMC window, expand Active Directory Users And Computers and Domain$y$ (where $y$ is the domain number), if they are not already expanded, and then select OU$z$ (where $z$ is your student number).

3. On the Action menu, click Delegate Control.

4. On the Delegation Of Control Wizard page, click Next.

5. On the Users Or Groups page, click Add.

6. In the Select Users, Computers, Or Groups dialog box, double-click User$z$, and then click OK.

7. On the Users Or Groups page, click Next.

8. On the Tasks To Delegate page, in the Delegate The Following Common Tasks list, select the check box next to Reset Passwords On User Accounts, and then click Next.

9. On the Completing The Delegation Of Control Wizard page, click Finish.

10. In the left pane of the MyCustomMMC window, right-click OU$z$, and then click Properties.

11. In the OU$z$ Properties dialog box, click the Security tab.

12. In the Security tab, click Advanced.

13. In the Access Control Settings For OU$z$ dialog box, in the Permission Entries list, select User$z$, and then click View/Edit.

    The Permission Entry For OU$z$ window appears.

    What permission is assigned to User$z$, and which objects does this permission apply to?

    _____

    _____

14. In the Permission Entry For OU$z$ dialog box, click OK.

15.  In the Access Control Settings For OU*z* dialog box, click OK.

16.  In the OU*z* Properties dialog box, click OK.

17.  Close the MyCustomMMC window.

You have successfully delegated to User*z* the permissions necessary to reset passwords for all users contained in OU*z*.

# Lab 13: Using TCP/IP Utilities

## Objectives

After completing this lab, you will be able to

- Use Nslookup.exe
- Use Ipconfig.exe
- Use Ping.exe
- Use Netstat.exe
- Use Nbtstat.exe

---

**Note** Completing this lab will help reinforce your learning from Chapter 13 of the textbook.

---

## Before You Begin

You will need to get the following information from your instructor before you begin this lab:

- The number assigned to your instructor's computer: $x$
- The number assigned to your classroom domain: $y$
- Your student number: $z$

**Estimated time to complete the lab: 30 minutes**

# Exercise 1
# Using TCP/IP Command-Line Utilities

In this exercise, you will use various Microsoft Windows 2000 Transmission Control Protocol/Internet Protocol (TCP/IP) command-line utilities, including Nslookup.exe, Ipconfig.exe, Ping.exe, Netstat.exe, and Nbtstat.exe.

▶    **To use Nslookup.exe**

1. Log on to Domain$y$ (where $y$ is the domain number) from your student computer as Student$z$ (where $z$ is your student number).

2. From the desktop, click Start, and then click Run.

3. In the Run dialog box, in the Open box, type **cmd** and then click OK.

4. At the command prompt, type **nslookup Instructor$x$.Domain$y$.com** (where $x$ is the number of your instructor's computer) and then press ENTER.

   What is the IP address assigned to your instructor's computer?

   _____


5. At the command prompt, type **nslookup Server$z$.Domain$y$.com** and then press ENTER.

   What is the IP address assigned to your student computer?

   _____


   Leave the command prompt window open for the next procedure.

   You have successfully used Nslookup.exe to look up the Internet Protocol (IP) address of your instructor's computer and the IP address of your student computer.

► **To use Ipconfig.exe**

At the command prompt, type **ipconfig /all** and then press ENTER.

Use the information displayed by Ipconfig.exe to fill in the information requested below. (You might have to use your mouse to scroll up or down through the output generated by Ipconfig.exe to complete this task.)

Host name                          _____

Primary DNS suffix                 _____

IP address                         _____

Subnet mask                        _____

DNS Server                         _____

Leave the command prompt window open for the next procedure.

You have successfully used Ipconfig.exe to view the IP address configuration information on your computer.

► **To use Ping.exe**

1. To use Ping.exe to verify that the TCP/IP stack is installed and working on your student computer, at the command prompt, type **ping 127.0.0.1** and then press ENTER.

   You should receive four replies from 127.0.0.1. The four replies indicate that TCP/IP is working correctly on your computer.

2. To use Ping.exe to verify that your IP address is correctly assigned, at the command prompt, type **ping *youripaddress*** (where *youripaddress* is the IP address of your computer, as reported by Ipconfig.exe in the previous procedure).

   You should receive four replies from your computer's IP address.

3. To use Ping.exe to verify that your computer can communicate with its assigned Domain Name System (DNS) server, at the command prompt, type **ping *yourdnsserver*** (where *yourdnsserver* is the IP address of your computer's DNS server, as reported by Ipconfig.exe in the previous procedure).

   You should receive four replies from the IP address of your DNS server. This indicates that you can send and receive IP traffic to and from your DNS server.

   Leave the command prompt window open for the next procedure.

You have successfully used Ping.exe to verify that TCP/IP is installed and configured correctly on your student computer and to verify that your student computer can communicate with your classroom's DNS server.

▶ **To use Netstat.exe**

1. To view the routing table on your student computer, at the command prompt, type **netstat -r** (the -r parameter is used to display the local computer's routing table), and then press ENTER.

   Are any persistent routes configured on your computer?

   _____

2. To view detailed network traffic statistics, at the command prompt, type **netstat -s** and then press ENTER.

   Leave the command prompt window open for the next procedure.

You have successfully used Netstat.exe to view the routing table and detailed network traffic statistics on your computer.

▶ **To use Nbtstat.exe**

1. To view the list of NetBIOS names registered on your student computer, at the command prompt, type **nbtstat -n** and then press ENTER.

   Your computer's NetBIOS Local Name Table is displayed. Notice that many of the names are registered multiple times, each with a different number in brackets after the name. The numbers represent specific services on the computer. For example, 00 is associated with the workstation service, 03 is associated with the messenger service, and 20 is associated with the server service.

2. To view the list of NetBIOS names registered on your instructor's computer, type **nbtstat -a Instructor*x*** (where *x* is the number of your instructor's computer), and then press ENTER.

3. At the command prompt, type **exit** and then press ENTER.

You have successfully used Nbtstat.exe to view the list of NetBIOS names registered on your computer and on your instructor's computer.

# Lab 14: Installing and Configuring DHCP

## Objectives

After completing this lab, you will be able to

- Install the Dynamic Host Configuration Protocol (DHCP) Server service on a computer running Microsoft Windows 2000 Server
- Authorize a DHCP server in the Active Directory service
- Create a scope on a DHCP server
- Configure scope options on a DHCP server
- Activate a scope on a DHCP server
- Deactivate a scope on a DHCP server
- Disable the DHCP Server service on a computer running Windows 2000 Server

---

**Note** Completing this lab will help reinforce your learning from Chapter 14 of the textbook.

---

## Before You Begin

You will need to get the following information from your instructor before you begin this lab:

- The number assigned to your classroom domain: $y$
- Your student number: $z$

**Estimated time to complete the lab: 50 minutes**

# Exercise 1
# Installing and Authorizing a DHCP Server

In this exercise, you will install the DHCP Server service on your student computer. Then you will authorize your DHCP server in Active Directory.

▶ **To install a DHCP server**

1. Log on to Domain*y* (where *y* is the domain number) from your student computer as Student*z* (where *z* is your student number).

2. From the desktop, click Start, point to Settings, and then click Control Panel.

3. In the Control Panel dialog box, double-click Add/Remove Programs.

4. In the Add/Remove Programs window, click Add/Remove Windows Components.

5. On the Windows Components Wizard page, in the Components list, select Networking Services, and then click Details.

6. In the Networking Services dialog box, in the Subcomponents Of Networking Services list, select the Dynamic Host Configuration Protocol (DHCP) check box, and then click OK.

7. On the Windows Components Wizard page, click Next.

   A Configuring Components page is displayed while DHCP is being installed.

8. On the Completing The Windows Components Wizard page, click Finish.

9. In the Add/Remove Programs dialog box, click Close.

10. Close Control Panel.

You have successfully installed the DHCP Server service on your student computer.

▶ **To authorize your DHCP server in Active Directory**

1. From the desktop, click Start, point to Programs, point to Administrative Tools, and then click DHCP.

2. In the DHCP window, in the left pane, right-click DHCP, and then click Add Server.

3. In the left pane of the DHCP window, click the name of your server.

   What icon appears on top of the server icon next to your computer name?

   _____

   What does this icon indicate?

   _____

4. In the DHCP window, in the left pane, right-click DHCP, and then click Manage Authorized Servers.

5. In the Manage Authorized Servers dialog box, click Authorize.

6. In the Authorize DHCP Server dialog box, in the Name Or IP Address box, type **Server**$z$ (where $z$ is your student number), and then click OK.

7. In the DHCP message box, click Yes to authorize your server.

   Notice that your server is now listed in the Authorized DHCP Servers list, along with your instructor's computer and other student computers.

8. In the Manage Authorized Servers dialog box, click Close.

9. In the DHCP window, on the Action menu, click Refresh.

   The icon on top of the server icon next to your computer name should have changed into a circle with a green arrow that points up, indicating that your DHCP server is authorized.

   If this is not the case, repeat this step every minute or so until the arrow changes from red to green. This process could take several minutes.

You have successfully authorized your DHCP server in Active Directory.

# Exercise 2
# Creating, Configuring, and Activating a Scope

In this exercise, you will create a scope, configure scope options, and then activate the scope.

▶   **To create a scope**

1. In the left pane of the DHCP window, right-click your computer name, and then click New Scope.

2. In the New Scope Wizard, on the Welcome To The New Scope Wizard page, click Next.

3. On the Scope Name page, in the Name box, type **10.240.z.0** (where *z* is your student number).

4. In the Description box, type **Scope for the 10.240.z.0 subnet** and then click Next.

5. On the IP Address Range page, in the Start IP Address box, type **10.240.z.1**.

6. In the End IP Address box, type **10.240.z.254**.

7. In the Length box, type **24** and then click Next.

8. On the Add Exclusions page, in the Start IP Address box, type **10.240.z.1**.

9. In the End IP Address box, type **10.240.z.10** and click Add, and then click Next.

10. On the Lease Duration page, click Next.

11. On the Configure DHCP Options page, select No, I Will Configure These Options Later, and then click Next.

12. On the Completing The New Scope Wizard page, click Finish.

You have successfully created a new scope.

▶   **To configure scope options**

1. In the left pane of the DHCP window, expand the scope you just created, and then select Scope Options.

    Read the description of Scope Options displayed in the right pane of the window.

2. In the left pane of the DHCP window, right-click Scope Options, and then click Configure Options.

3. In the Scope Options dialog box, in the Available Options list, select the 003 Router check box.

4. In the IP Address box, type **10.240.z.1** (where *z* is your student number), and then click Add.

5. In the Scope Options dialog box, in the Available Options list, select the 006 DNS Servers check box.

6. In the IP Address box, type **10.240.0.10** and then click Add.

7. In the Scope Options dialog box, in the Available Options list, select the 015 DNS Domain Name check box.

8. In the String Value box, type **Domainy.com** (where *y* is the domain number).

9. In the Scope Options dialog box, in the Available Options list, select the 044 WINS/NBNS Servers check box.

10. In the IP Address box, type **10.240.0.10** and then click Add.

11. In the Scope Options dialog box, in the Available Options list, select the 046 WINS/NBT Node Type check box.

12. In the Byte box, type **0x8** over the existing text, and then click OK.

    What information is listed in the right pane of the DHCP window?

    _____

    _____

    _____

    _____

    _____

You have successfully configured the most commonly used DHCP scope options.

▶ **To activate a scope**

In the left pane of the DHCP window, right-click the scope you just created and configured, and then click Activate.

Notice that the down-pointing red arrow disappears when you activate the scope.

You have successfully activated the scope.

# Exercise 3
# Deactivating a Scope and Disabling the DHCP Server Service

In this exercise, you will deactivate the scope you created and then disable the DHCP Server service on your computer.

▶ **To deactivate a scope**

1. In the left pane of the DHCP window, right-click the scope you just created and configured, and then click Deactivate.

2. In the DHCP message box, click Yes to disable the scope.

3. Close the DHCP window.

You have successfully deactivated the scope.

▶ **To disable the DHCP Server service on your computer**

1. From the desktop, right-click My Computer, and then click Manage.

2. In the left pane of the Computer Management window, expand Services And Applications, and then click Services.

3. In the right pane of the Computer Management window, right-click DHCP Server, and then click Stop.

4. In the right pane of the Computer Management window, right-click DHCP Server, and then click Properties.

5. In the DHCP Server Properties dialog box, in the Startup Type box, select Disabled, and then click OK.

6. Close the Computer Management window.

You have successfully deactivated the scope you created and disabled the DHCP Server service on your student computer.

# Lab 15: Using LMHOSTS Files and WINS

## Objectives

After completing this lab, you will be able to

- Create and edit an LMHOSTS file on a computer running Microsoft Windows 2000
- View the local Network Basic Input/Output System (NetBIOS) name cache using Nbtstat.exe
- Install Windows Internet Name Service (WINS)
- Configure WINS clients
- View WINS registrations by using the WINS console

---

**Note** Completing this lab will help reinforce your learning from Chapter 15 of the textbook.

---

## Before You Begin

You will need to get the following information from your instructor before you begin this lab:

- The number assigned to your instructor's computer: $x$
- The number assigned to your classroom domain: $y$
- Your student number: $z$

**Estimated time to complete the lab: 40 minutes**

# Exercise 1
# Creating and Editing an LMHOSTS File

In this exercise, you will use Microsoft Notepad to create and edit an LMHOSTS file on your student computer. You will also use Nbtstat.exe to view the contents of the local NetBIOS name cache.

▶   **To create and edit an LMHOSTS file**

1. Log on to Domain$y$ (where $y$ is the domain number) from your student computer as Student$z$ (where $z$ is your student number).

2. From the desktop, click Start, point to Programs, point to Accessories, and then click Notepad.

3. In the Untitled – Notepad window, type the following information. (Replace $x$ with the number assigned to your instructor's computer, and replace $y$ with the number assigned to your classroom domain.)

    **10.0.$x$.100    Instructor$x$    #PRE #DOM:Domain$y$**

4. In the Untitled – Notepad window, on the File menu, click Save As.

5. In the Save As dialog box, double-click My Computer, double-click Local Disk (C:), double-click Winnt, double-click System32, double-click Drivers, and then double-click Etc.

6. In the Save As dialog box, in the File Name box, type **Lmhosts** and then click Save.

7. Close Notepad.

8. From the desktop, click Start, and then click Run.

9. In the Run dialog box, in the Open box, type **cmd** and then click OK.

10. At the command prompt, change to the folder containing the Lmhosts file by typing **cd \Winnt\System32\Drivers\Etc** and then pressing ENTER.

11. At the command prompt, rename the Lmhosts.txt file to Lmhosts by typing **ren Lmhosts.txt Lmhosts** and then pressing ENTER.

    This action was necessary because Notepad automatically added a .txt extension to the file when it was saved. This renames the Lmhosts.txt file as Lmhosts.

12. At the command prompt, type **dir** and then press ENTER.

    Which files are in this folder?

    _____

    _____

    _____

13. At the command prompt, type **exit** and then press ENTER.

You have successfully created and edited an LHMOSTS file on your student computer.

▶ **To view the local NetBIOS name cache using Nbtstat.exe**

1. From the desktop, click Start, and then click Run.

2. In the Run dialog box, in the Open box, type **cmd** and then click OK.

3. At the command prompt, type **nbtstat -c** (the -c option is used to display the computer's NetBIOS name cache), and then press ENTER.

    Your computer's NetBIOS name cache appears.

    What entries are listed in your computer's NetBIOS name cache?

    _____

    _____

    _____

4. At the command prompt, type **nbtstat -R** and then press ENTER.

**Note**  Be sure to type the command in step 4 with a capital R.

    This clears your computer's NetBIOS name cache. It then loads all entries in your LMHOSTS file that are marked with the #PRE option into your NetBIOS name cache.

5. At the command prompt, type **nbtstat -c** and then press ENTER.

    Your computer's NetBIOS name cache appears.

    What entries are listed in your computer's NetBIOS name cache?

    _____

    _____

    _____

    _____

    _____

6. At the command prompt, type **exit** and then press ENTER.

You have successfully used Nbtstat.exe to view the local NetBIOS name cache and to clear the NetBIOS name cache and then load the #PRE entries from the LMHOSTS file. Then you used Nbtstat.exe to view the new entries in the cache.

# Exercise 2
# Installing WINS and Configuring WINS Clients

In this exercise, you will install WINS on your student computer and then configure your computer as a WINS client. You will also use the WINS console to view the active registrations on your WINS server.

▶ **To install WINS**

1. From the desktop, click Start, point to Settings, and then click Control Panel.

2. In Control Panel, double-click Add/Remove Programs.

3. In the Add/Remove Programs dialog box, click Add/Remove Windows Components.

4. On the Windows Components page, in the Components list, click Networking Services, and then click Details.

5. In the Networking Services dialog box, in the Subcomponents Of Networking Services list, select the Windows Internet Name Service (WINS) check box, and then click OK.

6. On the Windows Components page, click Next.

   The Configuring Components window is displayed as the needed files are copied.

7. In the Insert Disk message box, click OK.

8. In the Files Needed dialog box, in the Copy Files From box, type **\\Instructor*x*\W2000srv\I386** (where *x* is the number of your instructor's computer), and then click OK.

   This will cause your computer to copy the necessary files over the network from your instructor's computer.

9. On the Completing The Windows Components Wizard page, click Finish.

10. In the Add/Remove Programs dialog box, click Close.

11. Close Control Panel.

You have successfully installed WINS on your student computer.

▶ **To configure your computer as a WINS client**

1. From the desktop, right-click My Network Places, and then click Properties.

2. In the Network And Dial-Up Connections window, right-click Local Area Connection, and then click Properties.

3. In the Local Area Connection Properties dialog box, in the Components Checked Are Used By This Connection list, double-click Internet Protocol (TCP/IP).

4. In the Internet Protocol (TCP/IP) Properties dialog box, click Advanced.

5. In the Advanced TCP/IP Settings dialog box, click the WINS tab.

6. In the WINS tab, click Add.

7. In the TCP/IP WINS Server dialog box, in the WINS server box, type your computer's Internet Protocol (IP) address, **10.0.x.z** (where $x$ is the number of your instructor's computer and $z$ is your student number), and then click Add.

8. In the Advanced TCP/IP Settings dialog box, click OK.

9. In the Internet Protocol (TCP/IP) Properties dialog box, click OK.

10. In the Local Area Connection Properties dialog box, click OK.

11. Close the Network And Dial-Up Connections window.

You have successfully configured your student computer as its own WINS client.

▶ **To view the active registrations on your WINS server**

1. From the desktop, click Start, point to Programs, point to Administrative Tools, and then click WINS.

    The WINS console opens.

2. In the left pane of the WINS console, click the plus sign (+) next to your computer's name, and then click Active Registrations.

3. On the Action menu, click Find By Owner.

4. In the Find By Owner dialog box, click This Owner, and then click Find Now.

    What registrations are listed on your WINS server?

    _____

    _____

    _____

    _____

    _____

    Why are no other computers on your network registered with your WINS server?

    _____

    _____

5. Close the WINS console.

You have successfully viewed the WINS registrations on your student computer.

# Lab 16: Managing DNS

## Objectives

After completing this lab, you will be able to

- Install the Domain Name System (DNS) Server service
- Delegate a zone
- Create a zone
- Configure a zone for dynamic updates
- Create resource records
- Query the DNS server
- View the DNS server log

---

**Note** Completing this lab will help reinforce your learning from Chapter 16 of the textbook.

---

## Before You Begin

You will need to get the following information from your instructor before you begin this lab:

- The number assigned to your instructor's computer: $x$
- The number assigned to your classroom domain: $y$
- Your student number: $z$

**Estimated time to complete the lab: 60 minutes**

# Exercise 1
# Installing the DNS Server Service

In this exercise, you will use Add/Remove Programs in Control Panel to install the DNS Server service on your student computer.

▶ **To install the DNS Server service**

1. Log on to Domain*y* (where *y* is domain number) from your student computer as Student*z* (where *z* is your student number).

2. From the desktop, click Start, point to Settings, and then click Control Panel.

3. In Control Panel, double-click Add/Remove Programs.

4. On the Add/Remove Programs page, click Add/Remove Windows Components.

5. On the Windows Components page, select Networking Services, and then click Details.

6. In the Networking Services dialog box, in the Subcomponents Of Networking Services list, select the Domain Name System (DNS) check box, and then click OK.

7. On the Windows Components page, click Next.

   The Configuring Components window is displayed as the needed files are copied.

8. In the Insert Disk message box, click OK.

9. In the Files Needed dialog box, in the Copy Files From box, type **\\Instructor*x*\W2000srv\I386** (where *x* is the number of your instructor's computer), and then click OK.

   This will cause your computer to copy the necessary files over the network from your instructor's computer.

10. On the Completing The Windows Components Wizard page, click Finish.

11. In the Add/Remove Programs dialog box, click Close.

12. Close Control Panel.

You have successfully installed the DNS Server service on your student computer.

# Exercise 2
# Delegating, Creating, and Configuring a Zone

In this exercise, you will use the DNS console to delegate a zone, and then you will create a new zone and configure it for dynamic updates.

▶    **To delegate a zone**

1. From the desktop, click Start, point to Programs, point to Administrative Tools, and then click DNS.

2. In the DNS window, in the left pane, right-click DNS, and then click Connect To Computer.

3. In the Select Target Computer dialog box, select The Following Computer; then in the text box, type **Instructor*x*.Domain*y*.com** (where *x* is the number of your instructor's computer and *y* is the domain number); and then click OK.

4. In the DNS window, in the left pane, expand Instructor*x* and Forward Lookup Zones, and then click Domain*y*.

5. On the Action menu, click New Delegation to launch the New Delegation Wizard.

6. On the Welcome To The New Delegation Wizard page, click Next.

7. On the Delegated Domain Name page, in the Delegated Domain box, type **Subdomain*z*** (where *z* is your student number), and then click Next.

8. On the Name Servers page, click Add.

9. In the New Resource Record dialog box, in the Server Name text box, type **Server*z*.Domain*y*.com**, click Resolve, and then click OK.

10. In the New Delegation Wizard, on the Name Servers page, click Next.

11. On the Completing The New Delegation Wizard page, click Finish.

You have successfully delegated a zone.

▶    **To create a new zone on your student computer**

1. In the DNS window, in the left pane, click the minus sign (-) next to Instructor*x* (where *x* is the number of your instructor's computer), click the plus sign (+) next to the name of your student computer, and then click Forward Lookup Zones.

2. On the Action menu, click New Zone.

3. In the New Zone Wizard, on the Welcome To The New Zone Wizard page, click Next.

4. On the Zone Type page, select Standard Primary, and then click Next.

5. On the Zone Name page, in the Name text box, type
   **Subdomain*z*.Domain*y*.com** (where *z* is your student number and *y* is the
   domain number), and then click Next.

6. On the Zone File page, click Next.

7. On the Completing The New Zone Wizard page, click Finish.

You have successfully created a new zone on your student computer.

▶ **To configure a zone for dynamic updates**

1. In the DNS window, in the right pane, double-click the new zone you just
   created.

2. On the Action menu, click Properties.

3. In the Subdomain*z*.Domain*y*.com Properties dialog box (where *z* is your
   student number and *y* is the domain number), in the Allow Dynamic Updates
   list, select Yes, and then click OK.

4. Close the DNS window.

You have successfully configured the new zone to allow dynamic updates.

# Exercise 3
# Creating Resource Records

In this exercise, you will use the DNS console to create resource records in a zone.

▶   **To create resource records**

1. From the desktop, click Start, point to Programs, point to Administrative Tools, and then click DNS.

2. In the DNS window, expand Server$z$ (where $z$ is your student number) and Forward Lookup Zones (if they are not already expanded), and then click Subdomain$z$.Domain$y$.com (where $z$ is your student number and $y$ is the number of your classroom domain).

3. On the Action menu, click New Host.

4. In the New Host dialog box, in the Name box, type **Server$z$**; then in the IP Address box, type **10.0.$x$.$z$** (where $x$ is the number of your instructor's computer and $z$ is your student number), and then click Add Host.

5. In the DNS message box, click OK.

6. In the New Host dialog box, click Done.

7. On the Action menu, click New Alias.

8. In the New Resource Record dialog box, in the Alias Name box, type **Student$z$**; then in the Fully Qualified Name For Target Host text box, type **Server$z$.Subdomain$z$.Domain$y$.com** and then click OK.

9. Close the DNS window.

You have successfully created a Host record and an Alias record in the DNS zone you created in Exercise 2.

# Exercise 4
# Querying the DNS Server and Viewing the DNS Server Log

In this exercise, you will use the DNS snap-in in Computer Management to query your DNS server, and then you will use Event Viewer to view the DNS Server log on your instructor's computer.

▶    **To query the DNS server and view the DNS server log**

1.  From the desktop, right-click My Computer, and then click Manage.

2.  In the Computer Management window, in the left pane, expand Services And Applications and DNS, right-click Server*z* (where *z* is your student number), and then click Properties.

3.  In the Server*z* Properties dialog box, in the Monitoring tab, select the A Simple Query Against This DNS Server check box, and then click Test Now.

---

**Important**  Do not select the A Recursive Query To Other DNS Servers check box. A recursive query will fail unless your instructor has configured your classroom computers with full access to the Internet.

---

What are the test results?

_____

4.  In the Server*z* Properties dialog box, click OK.

5.  In the Computer Management window, in the left pane, right-click Computer Management (Local), and then click Connect To Another Computer.

6.  In the Select Computer dialog box, double-click the name of your instructor's computer.

7.  In the Computer Management dialog box, in the left pane, expand System Tools and Event Viewer, and then click DNS Server.

8.  In the right pane, double-click one of the events that is listed.

What is the description for the event?

_____

_____

_____

9.  In the Event Properties dialog box, click OK.

10.  Close the Computer Management window.

You have successfully performed a query against your DNS server and viewed the details for a DNS event in Event Viewer.

# Lab 17: Managing Internet Information Services

## Objectives

After completing this lab, you will be able to

- Install the File Transfer Protocol (FTP) Server component
- Create a new Web site
- Create a virtual directory by using the Microsoft Internet Information Services snap-in
- Create a virtual directory by using Web Sharing
- Redirect a directory to another Uniform Resource Locator (URL)
- Secure a Web site
- Configure a Web site to use Secure Sockets Layer (SSL)

---

**Note** Completing this lab will help reinforce your learning from Chapter 17 of the textbook.

---

## Before You Begin

This lab is dependent on Lab 2, Lab 4, Lab 5, and Lab 16. Lab 2, Lab 4, Lab 5, and Lab 16 must be completed before you begin this lab.

You will need to get the following information from your instructor before you begin this lab:

- The number assigned to your instructor's computer: $x$
- The number assigned to your classroom domain: $y$
- Your student number: $z$

**Estimated time to complete the lab: 2 hours 10 minutes**

# Exercise 1
# Installing the File Transfer Protocol (FTP) Server Component

In this exercise, you will use the Add/Remove Programs tool in Control Panel to install the File Transfer Protocol (FTP) Server component on your student computer.

▶ **To install the File Transfer Protocol (FTP) Server component**

1. Log on to Domain*y* (where *y* is the domain number) from your student computer as Student*z* (where *z* is your student number).

2. From the desktop, click Start, point to Settings, and then click Control Panel.

3. In Control Panel, double-click Add/Remove Programs.

4. In the Add/Remove Programs dialog box, click Add/Remove Windows Components.

5. In the Windows Components Wizard dialog box, in the Components list, select Internet Information Services (IIS), and then click Details.

6. In the Internet Information Services (IIS) dialog box, select the File Transfer Protocol (FTP) Server Component check box, and then click OK.

7. On the Windows Components page, click Next.

8. In the Insert Disk dialog box, click OK.

9. In the Files Needed dialog box, in the Copy Files From box, type **\\Instructor*x*\W2000srv\I386** (where *x* is the number assigned to your instructor's computer), and then click OK.

   This will cause your computer to copy the necessary files over the network from your instructor's computer.

10. On the Windows Components page, click Finish.

11. In the Add/Remove Programs dialog box, click Close.

12. Close Control Panel.

You have successfully installed the File Transfer Protocol (FTP) Server component on your student computer.

# Exercise 2
# Creating a New Web Site

In this exercise, you will create and copy the folders that will be used in this exercise and in the rest of the exercises in Lab 17. You will then use the Internet Information Services snap-in to create a new Web site. Then you will create a CNAME resource record on the classroom Domain Name System (DNS) server for the new site. Finally, you will test the new Web site by using Microsoft Internet Explorer.

▶ **To create and copy folders needed in this lab**

1. From the desktop, right-click My Computer, and then click Explore.

2. In the My Computer window, on the Tools menu, click Map Network Drive.

3. In the Map Network Drive dialog box, in the Folder box, type **\\Instructor*x*\LabFiles** (where *x* is the number assigned to your instructor's computer) and then click Finish.

4. Close the LabFiles On Instructor window when it appears.

5. In the My Computer window, in the left pane, click the drive labeled Labfiles On Instructor.

6. In the LabFiles On Instructor window, in the right pane, click the Accounting folder, then press and hold the CTRL key, then click the Marketing folder, then click the Sales folder, and then release the CTRL key.

7. In the LabFiles On Instructor window, on the Edit menu, click Copy.

8. In the LabFiles On Instructor window, in the left pane, expand Local Disk (C:), and then click the Inetpub folder.

9. In the Inetpub window, on the Edit menu, click Paste.

10. In the left pane of the Inetpub window, right-click the Inetpub folder, and then click Properties.

11. In the Inetpub Properties dialog box, select the Security tab.

12. In the Security tab, in the Name list, click the Everyone group; then in the Permissions box, click the Allow check box next to the Read & Execute permission, and then click OK.

13. In the Inetpub window, in the right pane, double-click the Wwwroot folder.

14. In the Wwwroot window, on the File menu, point to New, and then click Folder.

15. Name the new folder **ClassWeb** and then press ENTER.

16. Close the Wwwroot window.

You have successfully copied and created the folders that will be used throughout this lab.

▶    **To create a new Web site**

1. Click Start, point to Programs, point to Administrative Tools, and then click Internet Services Manager.

2. In the left pane of the Internet Information Services window, click the name of your computer.

   Notice that Default FTP Site, Default Web Site, Administration Web Site, and Default SMTP Virtual Server are listed in the right pane.

3. In the Internet Information Services window, from the Action menu, point to New, and then click Web Site.

4. In the Web Site Creation Wizard dialog box, on the Welcome To The Web Site Creation Wizard page, click Next.

5. On the Web Site Description page, in the Description box, type **Accountingz Web Site** (where $z$ is your student number), and then click Next.

6. On the IP Address And Port Settings page, in the Host Header For This Site box, type **Accountingz.Domainy.com** (where $y$ is the domain number), and then click Next.

7. On the Web Site Home Directory page, in the Path box, type **C:\Inetpub\Accounting** and then click Next.

8. On the Web Site Access Permissions page, click Next.

9. On the You Have Successfully Completed The Web Site Creation Wizard page, click Finish.

10. In the Internet Information Services window, in the left pane, right-click the Accountingz Web Site, and then click Properties.

11. In the Accountingz Web Site Properties dialog box, select the Documents tab.

12. In the Documents tab, click Add.

13. In the Add Default Document dialog box, in the Default Document Name box, type **Accounting.htm** and then click OK.

14. In the Accountingz Web Site Properties dialog box, in the Documents tab, in the Enable Default Document list, select Accounting.htm, then click the up arrow button on the left side of the dialog box two times to move Accounting.htm to the top of the list, and then click OK.

15. Close the Internet Information Services window.

You have successfully created and configured the Accountingz Web Site on your student computer.

▶ **To create an Alias (CNAME) resource record for the new Web site**

1. From the desktop, click Start, point to Programs, point to Administrative Tools, and then click DNS.

2. In the left pane of the DNS window, expand Instructor*x*.Domain*y*.com (where *x* is the number of your instructor's computer and *y* is the domain number), expand Forward Lookup Zones, and then click Domain*y*.com.

3. From the Action menu, click New Alias.

4. In the New Resource Record dialog box, in the Alias Name box, type **Accounting*z*** (where *z* is your student number); then in the Fully Qualified Name For Target Host box, type **Server*z*.Domain*y*.com** and then click OK.

   Notice that the Accounting alias is added to the right pane.

5. Close the DNS window.

You have successfully created an Alias (CNAME) resource record for the Web site you created earlier.

▶ **To test the new Web site**

1. From the desktop, click Start, and then click Run.

2. In the Run dialog box, in the Open box, type **http:// accounting*z*.domain*y*.com** (where *z* is your student number and *y* is the domain number), and then click OK.

   Internet Explorer opens to a Web page that states "Welcome to the Accounting Web Site."

3. Close Internet Explorer.

You have successfully created, configured, and tested your new Web site.

# Exercise 3
# Creating Virtual Directories and Redirecting a Directory to Another URL

In this exercise, you will use the Internet Information Services snap-in to create a virtual Web directory and then use Web Sharing to create another virtual directory. Next you will redirect requests for the ClassWeb directory to the ClassWeb virtual server on the instructor's computer. Finally, you will use Internet Explorer to test your virtual directories.

▶ **To create a virtual directory by using the Internet Information Services snap-in**

1. Log on to Domain*y* (where *y* is the domain number) from your student computer as Student*z* (where *z* is your student number).

2. From the desktop, click Start, point to Programs, point to Administrative Tools, and then click Internet Services Manager.

3. In the Internet Information Services window, in the left pane, click the plus sign (+) next to your computer name, right-click Default Web Site, point to New, and then click Virtual Directory.

4. In the Virtual Directory Creation Wizard, on the Welcome To The Virtual Directory Creation Wizard page, click Next.

5. On the Virtual Directory Alias page, in the Alias box, type **sales** and then click Next.

6. On the Web Site Content Directory page, in the Directory box, type **C:\Inetpub\Sales** and then click Next.

7. On the Access Permissions page, click Next.

8. On the You Have Successfully Completed The Virtual Directory Creation Wizard page, click Finish.

9. In the Internet Information Services window, in the left pane, click Default Web Site.

   Notice that a virtual directory named Sales is listed in the right pane.

10. Close the Internet Information Services window.

You have successfully created the Sales virtual directory by using the Internet Information Services snap-in.

▶ **To create a virtual directory by using Web Sharing**

1. From the desktop, right-click My Computer, and then click Explore.

2. In Windows Explorer, expand Local Disk (C:), expand the Inetpub folder, right-click the Marketing folder, and then click Properties.

3. In the Marketing Properties dialog box, click the Web Sharing tab.

4. In the Web Sharing tab, click Share This Folder.

5. In the Edit Alias dialog box, click OK.

6. In the Marketing Properties dialog box, click OK.

7. Close Windows Explorer.

You have successfully created the Marketing virtual directory by using Web Sharing.

▶ **To redirect requests for a directory to another URL**

1. From the desktop, click Start, point to Programs, point to Administrative Tools, and then click Internet Services Manager.

2. In the Internet Information Services window, in the left pane, click the plus sign (+) next to your computer name, expand Default Web Site, right-click the ClassWeb folder, and then click Properties.

3. In the ClassWeb Properties dialog box, in the Directory tab, select A Redirection To A URL.

4. In the Redirect To: box, type **http://classweb.domainy.com** (where $y$ is the domain number), and then click OK.

5. Close the Internet Information Services window.

You have successfully redirected requests for the ClassWeb folder to the ClassWeb Web site on your instructor's computer.

▶ **To test your virtual directories**

1. From the desktop, double-click Internet Explorer.

2. In the Internet Explorer window, in the Address box, type **http://localhost/sales** and then press ENTER.

   A Web page that states "Welcome to the Sales Web Site" appears.

3. In the Internet Explorer window, in the Address box, type **http://localhost/marketing** and then press ENTER.

   A Web page that states "Welcome to the Marketing Web Site" appears.

4. In the Internet Explorer window, in the Address box, type **http://localhost/classweb** and then press ENTER.

   A Web page that states "Welcome to the Classroom Web Site" appears.

   What URL is displayed in the Address box?

   _____

5. Close Internet Explorer.

You have successfully tested your virtual directories.

# Exercise 4
# Securing the Accounting Web Site and Configuring It to Use Secure Sockets Layer

In this exercise, you will configure the Accounting Web Site to use Integrated Windows authentication and to accept requests only from computers on the same subnet as the Web server, and then you will configure that Web site to use SSL. Finally, you will test the security on the Accounting Web Site by using Internet Explorer.

▶  **To secure the Accounting Web Site and configure it to use SSL**

1. Log on to Domain*y* (where *y* is the domain number) from your student computer as Student*z* (where *z* is your student number).

2. From the desktop, click Start, point to Programs, point to Administrative Tools, and then click Internet Services Manager.

3. In the Internet Information Services window, in the left pane, click the plus sign (+) next to your computer name, right-click Accounting*z* Web Site, and then click Properties.

4. In the Accounting*z* Web Site Properties dialog box, click the Directory Security tab.

5. In the Directory Security tab, in the Anonymous Access And Authentication Control box, click Edit.

6. In the Authentication Methods dialog box, clear the Anonymous Access check box, ensure that the Integrated Windows Authentication check box is selected, and then click OK.

7. In the Accounting*z* Web Site Properties dialog box, in the Directory Security tab, in the IP Address And Domain Name Restrictions dialog box, click Edit.

8. In the IP Address And Domain Name Restrictions dialog box, select Denied Access, and then click Add.

9. In the Grant Access On dialog box, select Group Of Computers; in the Network ID box, type **10.0.*x*.0** (where *x* is the number of your instructor's computer); then in the Subnet Mask box, type **255.255.255.0** and then click OK.

10. In the IP Address And Domain Name Restrictions dialog box, click OK.

11. In the Accounting*z* Web Site Properties dialog box, in the Directory Security tab, in the Secure Communications box, click Server Certificate.

12. On the Welcome To The Web Server Certificate Wizard page, click Next.

13. In the IIS Certificate Wizard, on the Server Certificate page, select Create A New Certificate, and then click Next.

14. On the Delayed Or Immediate Request page, select Send The Request Immediately To An Online Certification Authority, and then click Next.

15. On the Name And Security Settings page, click Next to accept the default settings for the certificate name and bit length.

16. On the Organization Information page, in the Organization box, type **Domainy**; then in the Organizational Unit box, type **OUz** and then click Next.

17. On the Your Site's Common Name page, in the Common Name box, type **Accountingz.Domainy.com** and then click Next.

18. On the Geographical Information page, in the State/Province box, type **Washington**; then in the City/Locality box, type **Redmond** and then click Next.

19. On the Choose A Certification Authority page, in the Certification Authorities list, select Instructor*x*.Domainy.com\Domainy, and then click Next.

20. On the Certificate Request Submission page, click Next.

21. On the Completing The Web Server Certificate Wizard page, click Finish.

22. In the Accounting*z* Web Site Properties dialog box, in the Directory Security tab, in the Secure Communications dialog box, click Edit.

23. In the Secure Communications dialog box, select the Require Secure Channel (SSL) check box, then select the Require 128-Bit Encryption check box, and then click OK.

24. In the Accounting*z* Web Site Properties dialog box, click the Web Site tab.

25. In the Web Site tab, in the SSL Port box, type **443** (the default port number for SSL communications); then in the IP Address box, select your computer's IP address, and then click OK.

26. Close the Internet Information Services window.

You have successfully secured the Accounting Web Site and configured it to use SSL.

▶  **To test the security on the Accounting Web Site**

1. From the desktop, double-click Internet Explorer.

2. In the Internet Explorer window, in the Address box, type **http://accoutingz.domainy.com** (where *z* is your student number and *y* is the domain number) and then press ENTER.

What information is displayed?

_____

_____

_____

3. In the Internet Explorer window, in the Address box, type **https://accoutingz.domainy.com** and then press ENTER.

4. In the Security Alert dialog box, click OK.

5. In the Enter Network Password window, authenticate to domainy as Studentz.

   A Web page is displayed that states "Welcome to the Accounting Web Site."

6. Close Internet Explorer.

You have successfully tested the security on the Accounting Web Site.

# Lab 18: Managing Remote Client Access

## Objectives

After completing this lab, you will be able to

- Configure and enable Routing and Remote Access as a remote access server
- Create and configure a remote access policy
- Configure a virtual private network (VPN) client connection and use it to connect to the remote access server
- Install and configure Terminal Services
- Install Terminal Services client software and connect to the Terminal Services server

---

**Note** Completing this lab will help reinforce your learning from Chapter 18 of the textbook.

---

## Before You Begin

This lab is dependent on Lab 8 and Lab 9. Lab 8 and Lab 9 must be completed before you begin this lab.

You will need to get the following information from your instructor before you begin this lab:

- The number assigned to your instructor's computer: $x$
- The number assigned to your classroom domain: $y$
- Your student number: $z$

**Estimated time to complete the lab: 1 hour 25 minutes**

# Exercise 1
# Configuring and Enabling Routing and Remote Access

In this exercise, you will use the Routing And Remote Access console to configure and enable Routing and Remote Access as a remote access server.

▶ **To configure and enable Routing and Remote Access**

1. Log on to Domain$y$ (where $y$ is the domain number) from your student computer as Student$z$ (where $z$ is your student number).

2. From the desktop, click Start, point to Programs, point to Administrative Tools, and then click Routing And Remote Access.

3. In the Routing And Remote Access window, in the left pane, right-click your computer name, and then click Configure And Enable Routing And Remote Access.

4. On the Welcome To The Routing And Remote Access Server Setup Wizard page, click Next.

5. On the Common Configurations page, select Remote Access Server, and then click Next.

6. On the Remote Client Protocols page, click Next.

7. On the IP Address Assignment page, select From A Specified Range Of Addresses, and then click Next.

8. On the Address Range Assignment page, click New.

9. In the New Address Range dialog box, in the Start IP Address box, type **10.$z$.0.101**; then in the Number Of Addresses box, type **10** and then click OK.

10. On the Address Range Assignment page, click Next.

11. On the Managing Multiple Remote Access Servers page, click Next.

12. On the Completing The Routing And Remote Access Server Setup Wizard page, click Finish.

13. In the Routing And Remote Access message box, click OK.

14. Close the Routing And Remote Access window.

You have successfully configured and enabled Routing and Remote Access as a remote access server.

# Exercise 2
# Creating and Configuring a Remote Access Policy

In this exercise, you will use the Routing And Remote Access console to create and configure a new remote access policy.

▶    **To create and configure a remote access policy**

1. From the desktop, click Start, point to Programs, point to Administrative Tools, and then click Routing And Remote Access.

2. In the Routing And Remote Access window, click the plus sign (+) next to your computer name, and then click Remote Access Policies.

3. On the Action menu, point to New, and then click Remote Access Policy.

4. In the Add Remote Access Policy dialog box, in the Policy Friendly Name box, type **Allow members of Global$z$ to dial in** (where $z$ is your student number), and then click Next.

5. In the Add Remote Access Policy dialog box, on the Conditions page, click Add.

6. In the Select Attribute dialog box, double-click Windows – Groups.

7. In the Groups dialog box, click Add.

8. In the Select Groups dialog box, in the Look In list, select Domain$y$.com (where $y$ is the domain number); then in the Name list, double-click Global$z$, and then click OK.

9. In the Groups dialog box, click OK.

10. In the Add Remote Access Policy dialog box, on the Conditions page, click Next.

11. On the Permissions page, select Grant Remote Access Permission, and then click Next.

12. On the User Profile page, click Finish.

13. In the Routing And Remote Access window, in the right pane, click the Allow Members Of Global$z$ To Dial In policy.

14. In the Routing And Remote Access window, on the Action menu, click Move Up.

    Notice that the Allow Members Of Global$z$ To Dial In policy is now at the top of the list and has an order number of 1.

15. Close the Routing And Remote Access window.

You have successfully created and configured a new remote access policy on your student computer.

# Exercise 3
# Configuring a VPN Client Connection and Connecting to the Remote Access Server

In this exercise, you will use the Network And Dial-Up Connections tool to configure a VPN client connection, and then you will use this connection to connect to the remote access server you configured and enabled in Exercise 1.

▶ **To configure a VPN client connection and use it to connect to the remote access server**

1. Log on to Domain*y* (where *y* is the domain number) from your student computer as Student*z* (where *z* is your student number).

2. From the desktop, right-click My Network Places, and then click Properties.

3. In the Network And Dial-Up Connections window, double-click Make New Connection.

4. In the Location Information dialog box, in the What Area Code (Or City Code) Are You In Now box, type **425** and then click OK.

---

**Note**  If you do not see the Location Information dialog box, skip to step 6.

---

5. In the Phone And Modem Options dialog box, click OK.

6. On the Welcome To The Network Connection Wizard page, click Next.

7. On the Network Connection Type page, select Connect To A Private Network Through The Internet, and then click Next.

8. On the Destination Address page, in the Host Name Or IP Address box, type **Server*z*.Domain*y*.com** and then click Next.

9. On the Connection Availability page, select For All Users, and then click Next.

10. On the Internet Connection Sharing page, click Next.

11. On the Completing The Network Connection Wizard page, click Finish.

12. In the Connect Virtual Private Connection dialog box, in the User Name box, type **User*z*** and type User*z*'s password in the Password box, and then click Connect.

13. In the Connection Complete message box, click OK.

14. In the Network And Dial-Up Connections window, right-click Virtual Private Connection, and then click Status.

   What is the status of the connection? How long has it had this status?

---

15. In the Virtual Private Connection Status dialog box, click Disconnect.

16. Close the Network And Dial-Up Connections window.

You have successfully configured a VPN client connection and used the connection to connect to a remote access server.

# Exercise 4
# Installing and Configuring Terminal Services

In this exercise, you will install and configure Terminal Services on your student computer.

► **To install and configure Terminal Services**

1. Log on to Domain*y* (where *y* is the domain number) from your student computer as Student*z* (where *z* is your student number).

2. From the desktop, click Start, point to Settings, and then click Control Panel.

3. In Control Panel, double-click Add/Remove Programs.

4. In the Add/Remove Programs dialog box, click Add/Remove Windows Components.

5. On the Windows Components page, in the Components list, select the Terminal Services check box, and then click Next.

6. On the Terminal Services Setup page, select Remote Administration Mode, and then click Next.

7. In the Insert Disk dialog box, click OK.

8. In the Files Needed dialog box, in the Copy Files From box, type **\\Instructor*x*\W2000srv\I386** (where *x* is the number of your instructor's computer), and then click OK.

   This will cause your computer to copy the necessary files over the network from your instructor's computer.

9. On the Completing The Windows Components Wizard page, click Finish.

10. In the System Settings Change message box, click Yes to restart your computer.

You have successfully installed and configured Terminal Services on your student computer.

# Exercise 5
# Installing Terminal Services Client Software and Connecting to the Terminal Services Server

In this exercise, you will install the Terminal Services client software on your student computer and then connect to the Terminal Services server.

▶ **To install the Terminal Services client software and connect to the Terminal Services server**

1. Log on to Domain*y* (where *y* is the domain number) from your student computer as Student*z* (where *z* is your student number).

2. From the desktop, right-click My Computer, and then click Explore.

3. In the My Computer window, expand Local Disk (C:), expand Winnt, expand System32, expand Clients, expand Tsclient, expand Net, click Win32, and then in the right pane, double-click Setup.

4. In the Terminal Services Client Setup dialog box, click Continue.

5. In the Name And Organization Information dialog box, in the Name box, type your name; then in the Organization box, type **Classroom** and then click OK.

6. In the Confirm Name And Organization Information dialog box, click OK.

7. In the License Agreement dialog box, click I Agree.

8. In the Terminal Services Client Setup dialog box, click the large button to start the installation.

9. In the Terminal Services Client Setup message box, click Yes to install the client software for all users of your student computer.

10. In the Terminal Services Client Setup message box, click OK.

11. Close the Win32 window.

12. Click Start, point to Programs, point to Terminal Services Client, and then click Terminal Services Client.

13. In the Terminal Services Client dialog box, in the Available Servers list, click Server*z*, and then click Connect.

14. In the Server*z* – Terminal Services Client dialog box, log on to your Terminal Services server as Student*z*.

    Logging on in the Terminal Services Client dialog box establishes a session with your terminal server and provides you with a desktop from your server that you have accessed by using Terminal Services.

15. In the Server*z* – Terminal Services Client screen, click Start, and then click Log Off Student*z*.

16. In the Log Off Windows message box, click Yes.

17. In the Terminal Services Client dialog box, click Cancel.

You have successfully installed the Terminal Services client software and used the client software to connect to a Terminal Services server.

# Lab 19: Backing Up System State Data

## Objectives

After completing this lab, you will be able to

- Back up System State data

---

**Note** Completing this lab will help reinforce your learning from Chapter 19 of the textbook.

---

## Before You Begin

You will need to get the following information from your instructor before you begin this lab:

- The number assigned to your classroom domain: $y$
- Your student number: $z$

---

**Note** A tape backup device is *not* required to perform this lab.

---

**Estimated time to complete the lab: 15 minutes**

# Exercise 1
# Backing Up System State Data

In this exercise, you will use the Microsoft Windows 2000 Backup program to back up the System State data on your student computer to a file.

▶ **To back up System State data**

1. Log on to Domain*y* (where *y* is the domain number) from your student computer as Student*z* (where *z* is your student number).

2. From the desktop, click Start, point to Programs, point to Accessories, point to System Tools, and then click Backup.

3. In the Backup dialog box, click the Backup tab.

4. In the Backup tab, in the left pane, select the System State check box, and then select System State.

   Which System State items are listed in the right pane?

   _____

   _____

   _____

   Which additional System State items would be listed in the right pane on a Windows 2000 domain controller?

   _____

   _____

5. In the Backup tab, in the Backup Destination list, select File.

**Note** This option might be dimmed on your student computer. If so, skip this step.

6. In the Backup tab, in the Backup Media Or File Name box, type **C:\SystemState.bkf** and then click Start Backup.

   This will cause the backup of your computer's System State data to be stored in a file named SystemState.bkf in the root of drive C.

7. In the Backup Job Information dialog box, select Replace The Data On The Media With This Backup, and then click Start Backup.

   A Backup Progress dialog box is displayed while the Backup program backs up the System State data on your student computer to the C:\SystemState.bkf file. The backup process takes a few minutes.

8. After the backup is completed, in the Backup Progress dialog box, click Report.

   Microsoft Notepad opens and displays the report. Notice the type of information that is included in the report.

9. Close Notepad.

10. In the Backup Progress dialog box, click Close.

11. Close the Backup dialog box.

You have successfully backed up the System State data on your student computer to a file.